THE SECRETS OF SUCCESSFUL TELESALES

Also by Alfred Tack

The Secrets of Successful Selling

THE SECRETS OF SUCCESSFUL TELESALES

Make every call count

Alfred Tack

VERMILION
LONDON

First published in the United Kingdom by Cedar in 1978.
This edition published in the United Kingdom in 2000 by Vermilion,
an imprint of Ebury Press.
Random House, 20 Vauxhall Bridge Road, London SW1V 2SA

Random House Australia (Pty) Limited
20 Alfred Street, Milsons Point, Sydney,
New South Wales 2061, Australia

Random House New Zealand Limited
18 Poland Road, Glenfield,
Auckland 10, New Zealand

Random House South Africa (Pty) Limited
Endulini, 5A Jubilee Road,
Parktown 2193, South Africa

Random House Group Limited Reg. No. 954009
www.randomhouse.co.uk

ISBN 009 185 605 1

Typeset in Baskerville by MATS, Southend-on-Sea, Essex
Printed and bound in Denmark by Nørhaven, Viborg

Papers used by Vermilion are natural, recyclable products
made from wood grown in sustainable forests.

Contents

CHAPTER 1

The Telephone Market

Deciding to buy a new car, I telephoned a British company for information.

Their receptionist told me the line to the salesperson was engaged and asked me whether I wanted to hold on or ring back. I held on.

Eventually I spoke to a salesperson and asked, 'Can you tell me the overall length and width of Model X?'

This simple question stumped him. He asked me to hold on while he found a brochure. Several minutes later, he returned to the telephone and gave me the dimensions, adding, 'Anything else you want to know?'

'No,' I answered.

'Okay, then. Goodbye.'

There was not the slightest effort on his part to gain my interest. Neither did he ask my name and address. Yet car manufacturers are always complaining about the difficulties of marketing during periods of credit restriction.

I wrote to another distributor of a well-known British car. The sales manager posted a catalogue to me in response to my request for details, but he did not enclose a covering letter – only a compliment slip. I heard no more from him.

Is this a diatribe against British manufacturers and distributors? Not at all. The distribution of foreign cars proved to be just as bad. The sales manager in charge of the distribution of an American car wrote a good letter which included the sentences:

A demonstration model is available, and I shall gladly arrange a test drive to suit your convenience. Should you require any further information, please don't hesitate to contact me.

I did not contact her –and she didn't contact me.

The letter from the distributor of a German car was signed by a PA per pro the production manager. Here is an extract:

. . . If, after studying the literature, you feel that you would like a demonstration, please don't hesitate to contact the writer, who will be pleased to make the necessary arrangements.

Here we have examples of inefficient salesmanship. It is a seller's job to try to convert every prospect into a buyer, and he or she should telephone every prospective buyer within 24 hours of receiving an enquiry.

Why don't they do so? Some are afraid to use the telephone; others treat it too casually. Many take the coward's way out and prefer to write letters rather than face up to a person-to-person call.

Avis achieved success in the car-hire world by claiming that, as No. 2 to Hertz, they had to try harder. They certainly did as far as telephone usage was concerned. The president of Avis had a separate telephone line specially installed in his office. He advertised the fact, and invited anyone with a complaint to telephone him direct. He didn't receive many calls, but his enlightened action brought the company a lot of publicity.

How different from the attitude of one of our leading appliance manufacturers.

A friend of mine purchased a dishwasher which did a first-class job. Having great difficulty in obtaining a small, easily-fitted replacement part from the supplier, she wrote a personal letter to the service manager of the appliance manufacturer. Although it was a letter of complaint, she went out of her way to mention that his firm used many different pieces of equipment manufactured by the appliance company, and had always been satisfied with their machines and service.

Ten days later, she received a compliment slip from the customer-relations department of the company advising her that a replacement had been sent.

Why couldn't the service manager have replied personally to my friend's letter or, better still, telephoned to show his concern about what had happened? He could then have apologised for not writing a letter and explained that the first priority was for the replacement part to be sent. He could have thanked my friend for the kind way in which she had written.

If he had taken this action, my friend would quickly have forgotten the bad service, but would have remembered for a long time the efficiency and courtesy of the service manager.

There are so many similar opportunities to increase sales and goodwill by better use of the telephone.

The Follow-up

It would seem obvious that enquiries, requests for brochures, and responses to advertising should be followed up quickly, yet this only happens in the most efficient companies. Often, the standard practice is either to post the brochure or to send the enquiry on to a salesperson to deal with. If an advertising campaign pulls well, salespeople may have more enquiries than they can handle quickly. The result is a delayed call and, perhaps, an order lost.

If there is the possibility of the salesperson's call being delayed, then it is more efficient to use the telephone as a follow-up. The advantage of this is twofold. The prospect's interest is maintained, and the telephone salesperson can evaluate the strength of the enquiry. It may be that it is so weak that it would not pay a salesperson to call at all; there are always a number of enquiries received from direct mail advertising shots and advertising campaigns which are of no value.

The telephone may be used:

(a) to make a sale;
(b) to make an appointment for a salesperson to call;
(c) to service the prospect until a salesperson can call;
(d) to check whether a brochure has arrived, or to evaluate the strength of the enquiry.

A tailor who ran a small business regularly advertised his made-to-measure sports jackets and trousers in a newspaper's *Saturday Postal Bargain* columns. On receipt of an enquiry, he would send patterns, and hope for an order. The response was poor, so he changed his policy. Five days after the patterns had been sent, he telephoned the prospect and explained fully the specialised service he was offering. The result was 80% conversion of enquiries into sales, against 25% previously. He now has a flourishing mail order business in men's wear.

A garage proprietor instituted a sales drive for tyres. Six months after a car was sold, either new or second-hand, his sales staff would telephone the customer to check on the tyre wear. If the customer told him that there was still good tread on the tyres, he would check again three months later. Sales of tyres increased 30%.

A wine merchant regularly telephones his customers advising them of special shipments of wine. The customers feel flattered, often purchase the wines, and also order other drinks at the same time.

Every marketing organisation should consider what additional business can be obtained by using the telephone for following up enquiries or selling extras to customers.

Keeping Out Competition

The marketing policy of a company supplying office computers is dynamic. They train their salespeople well and all enquiries are followed up within twenty-four hours. One of their best accounts is an insurance company, looked after by a senior salesperson.

After booking a repeat order for 24 new computers, he believed that he had satisfied their needs for several months ahead. However, five weeks after the new computers had been delivered, the accounts department needed an advanced word processing system.

A competitor from another computer company had been calling on the insurance company every month in the hope of getting some business from them. He called once more on the day the request was made for the new computer system.

He got the order, became very friendly with the buyer, obtained more business later, and then became firmly entrenched.

Too many marketing directors and sales staff believe that no one can take business away from accounts which they have had for years. They forget the age-old dictum,

Never forget a customer – never let a customer forget you.

The best way of maintaining contact and keeping competition at bay is to service customers regularly by telephone in between the salesperson's calls.

If this had been the policy of the company selling PCs, apparently so efficiently, they would have maintained their monopoly instead of having to share the business with a competitor.

In the consumer field, it is standard practice to telephone retailers for repeat business. It should also be a marketing tool for companies selling consumer durables and equipment.

The wise production manager inaugurates a system of regular follow-ups by telephone on all large quotations, knowing that competitors' quotations are also being considered.

Making Appointments

This is a five-star aid to salesmanship, and it is surprising that it is so neglected. Often a salesperson is left to make her own appointments in her own way, which may be the wrong way, because she is not trained in telephone techniques. More and more companies are, however, employing telephone sales staff to make appointments for their sales staff. It cannot be right for a highly paid salesperson to spend perhaps a full day every week making appointments for the following four days. It is far better to employ telephone sales people to make these appointments for the sales force. Each telesales person should be able to keep three salespeople fully booked with appointments.

When a company selling accounting software adopted this procedure, sales increased by 20%–but then, the salespeople were making 20% more contacts.

Evaluating Applicants
The standard procedure for engaging sales staff is to advertise the vacancy, consider letters sent in by applicants, select those whose qualifications line up with the job specification, and send them application forms. When these forms are returned and evaluated, selected salespeople are invited to attend an interview.

The expense of bringing salespeople long distances (it doesn't pay a production manager to travel many miles to interview one applicant) is considerable, and it can be time wasting. Under these circumstances, an initial telephone call can:

> enable the production manager to evaluate further the applicant's potential;
> enable the applicants to decide whether or not it is the type of job they want;
> save a wasted and expensive journey.

To Increase Goodwill
When there is a delivery problem, why wait until a

complaint is received? It is far better to telephone the customer and explain the reason for the delay.

A 'thank you' for a worthwhile order is always well received by a customer, because this courtesy is so unusual.

Rather than send out a printed invitation to view a new range of goods, why not telephone and make the invitation really personal.

If merchandise has to be substituted, it is better to telephone than to write a standard letter explaining the reason for this substitution.

The telephone can be used to give good news quickly to customers, or to explain why lines are out of stock.

Finding Dealers

Dealerships can be set up more quickly by telephone than by writing a letter to make the initial contact. A would-be dealer always appreciates a call from a top executive, and the franchise can often be closed on the telephone. If not, the salesperson will find it much easier to finalise the arrangements when she calls.

To Obtain Leads

Use your users is one of the oldest tags in selling. It still remains true. Your users are your best friends, and are often willing to supply leads if asked for them. When you service a customer by telephone, ensure that he is satisfied with his purchase by adding,

> 'Mr. Jones, I am sure you have a friend or business acquaintance who would also want . . .'

Wholesalers

The death-knell of wholesalers has been sounded

many times, but the efficient wholesaler can play a most important part in the marketing plan. Some wholesalers only wait for business to arrive, while others employ *order takers* who have little time to spare for selling.

The main service offered by a wholesaler is a quick replacement of stock. Efficient use of the telephone is essential for wholesale marketing. A trained operator can save the salesperson's time, allowing him to sell more profitable lines and increase turnover.

Selling Direct
The direct telephone selling market has grown at a phenomenal rate in recent years. Telesales staff sell magazine subscriptions, advertising, consumer goods, cosmetics, insurance (increases), cleaning services decorating, consumer durables, etc.

Save Writing a Letter or E-mail
It's cheaper and quicker to telephone.

Customer Reaction To New Products
Market research can be carried out more rapidly over the telephone.

Maintaining Contact With Service Engineers
Service engineers are notoriously bad users of time. Telephone checks are better than reports received three days after the event.

Credit Restrictions
When goods are held up because credit has been exceeded, a telephone call can do two things:

   (a) get the account paid;
   (b) get the goods flowing to the customer again.

To write a letter under these circumstances may result in the customer ignoring the letter and going to a competitor for similar goods.

To Rescind Cancellations
Salespeople often find it hard to reinstate orders. Sometimes they avoid making calls to dissatisfied customers, but a head office executive telephoning can often win them back.

Check on Advertising
Don't leave it to the advertising agent to tell you that the advertisement is brilliant. Check up yourself to make certain that the advertisement is appreciated by customers, dealers, and sales staff.

Enquiries
Get them to the salespeople quickly, by telephone. While a postman is sorting out the letters, another company could be booking the order.

Small Accounts
It often doesn't pay to send a salesperson to small traders. It does pay to keep those traders on the books by telephone selling.

Uncovered Territory
Cold canvass telephone calls on prospects trading in open territories can lead to a build-up of accounts which may warrant the allocation of the territory to a salesperson at a later date.

Selling the Extra
It sometimes isn't possible for a salesperson to sell all the extras at an initial sale. One of the companies in our group, Nu-aire Ltd., obtains 15% of service

contracts over the telephone.

Collecting Overdue Accounts

Credit control should be included in your overall marketing plan so that the cash flow can be maintained. Without a good cash flow, sales programmes may have to be cut. Collecting accounts by telephone is, therefore, a selling job.

Special Opportunities

The business columns in the national daily newspapers can be used to find leads. Executives who have been promoted to senior positions may require a new car, or they may be thinking about moving to a larger house or installing a swimming pool.

Seasons

The salesperson selling unit heating appliances can contact many more prospects by telephone during the month of September than he can ever do by personal calling.

The salesperson selling garden furniture can carry out similar cold canvass telephoning in early summer.

Weddings and Engagements

Newlyweds, or those about to be married, are always good prospects for furniture, houses, jewellery, clothing and travel.

New Factory Premises

Get in first by telephoning when a factory is being designed or built. It enables you to find and make the right contacts.

It is no use being second when selling vending

machines, canned music, freezers for cafeterias, office furniture and PCs.

There are many opportunities for increasing business by telephone selling. The market is wide open, waiting to be tapped.

CHAPTER 2

Everyone Sells

Scene: A general office

'Hello.'
'Can I speak to Ms. Brown, please?'
'Who is speaking?'
'I want to talk to Ms. Brown.'
'But I must know who's calling.'
'John Smith, of Smith's Pumps.'
'What are you calling about?'
'I have a price query.'
'Then you want the order department.'
'No, I want to speak to Ms. Brown.'
'Well, she isn't in yet.'
'When will she be in?'
'In about half an hour's time, I should think . . .'

And that employee, masquerading under the title of PA, doesn't believe he has a selling function.

Scene: A managing director's office

'Johnson here.'
'Good morning, Mr. Johnson. It's Bob White again, of White's Ltd. You will remember I spoke to you last week about the delivery of the steel partitioning. It still hasn't arrived.'
'Mr. White, I told you that we are, unfortunately, a little behind with deliveries and that you should take the matter up with Mr. Tilling.'
'I can't get a satisfactory response from Mr. Tilling.

That's why I am telephoning you.'

'It's not my department. You can't expect me to go chasing every order we get, can you?'

'No, but we're in real trouble, and your salesperson knew the position when I placed the order. We must have the partitioning fixed before most of the staff return from their holidays.'

'I'm sorry, we've all got our troubles. You really must deal with Mr. Tilling.'

'But I just told you –'

'Good God, man, what do you expect me to do, bring the wretched stuff myself?'

That managing director doesn't think he is concerned in any way with selling. He prides himself on being a highly efficient administrator.

Scene: A credit control department

'Mr. Green, unless we have your cheque by Friday, we will take proceedings.'

'What on earth do you mean? Your salesperson pestered me for months to open the account and said that two months' credit was normal.'

'It was, once. It isn't now. There's a squeeze on. I've written you three letters.'

'Your salesperson said it was routine.'

'I'm not concerned with what the salesperson said. My job is to collect, and I must have your cheque by Friday.'

And that credit control manager doesn't believe that she has a selling job to do.

Scene: A service department

'My washing machine has broken down again. Can you send a mechanic quickly?'

'Just a minute.'

'It's very urgent.'

'Everything's urgent. Hold on . . . Okay Mrs. Harris, I'll send someone next Friday-week.'

'But that's in ten days' time.'

'And that's doing you a favour. I have three mechanics away ill, and we're short of staff anyway.'

'But I have five children . . .'

'That's not my fault, Mrs. Harris. Ten days is the very best I can do.'

And that service manager doesn't believe he is in any way involved in selling.

All these examples are true. Only the names have been changed. They were sent to me in response to my request for examples of bad treatment over the telephone.

I sent out fifty letters, and thirty examples of inefficiency in telephone communication were returned to me. Nine other correspondents wrote to say that they had never had cause for complaint, and eleven did not reply.

Why is it that normally friendly and courteous people change when they use a telephone? Why is this allowed to happen in business?

Everyone in an organisation is a part of a marketing plan, and included in that plan must be telephone selling. One person can undo all the brilliant work of a salesperson in opening an account, or can hinder his or her negotiations for a large order.

One of our consultants working on an assignment was

discussing with the buyer of packaging material the products and services offered by various suppliers. During the conversation he asked the reason for the sharp drop in purchases from a well-known public company.

The buyer, a woman, answered, 'I hate telephoning *them*. No one ever seems interested. *They* always have that couldn't-care-less attitude.'

The significant words are *them* and *they*. What the buyer should have said was, *she* or *him*.

Because an individual had failed to appreciate his or her specific communication responsibilities, the whole organisation was condemned.

In the same way that many male car drivers believe that they are highly skilled, and some women consider themselves to be fashion-conscious, so the majority of people mislead themselves into believing that they know how to communicate efficiently by telephone. In consequence of this mistaken belief, some business executives are abrupt, considering that others waste time on the telephone. The psychological reason for their abruptness is often that the telephone gives them an opportunity of being in control without having to look someone straight in the eye. Others are garrulous and can never conclude a conversation until they have said several goodbyes. They believe they are showing courtesy and friendliness, when they are only proving their lack of knowledge of telephone techniques.

Then there are the people who mumble, or whose voices are indistinct because they hold the mouthpiece at arm's length.

The art of telephone communication in industry must be learned. Experience since childhood does not guarantee *telefficiency*. Experience may only result in the perpetuation of mistakes. Telephone communication does not come naturally to people. Joe Louis, heavyweight champion of the world from 1937-1948 and one of the all-time greats in boxing once said, 'People read that I was born with the movements of a panther. The truth is that I was a very clumsy kid. The footwork they called "cat sense" was something Chappie Blackburn drilled into me. That was learnt; it wasn't a "born" thing.'

Check
You can prove something for yourself right now, if the time is between 9 a.m. and 5 p.m.

Pick up your telephone and ring consecutively five different companies advertising their products or services in a newspaper or magazine, which include a telephone number in their advertisement. Ask for further details of the goods or services they are offering. In total, you will probably speak to fifteen different people at least – five telephone receptionists and five go-betweens who will then pass you on to five others who may come up with the right information. Try it. You won't prove me wrong. Yet these telesellers believe themselves to be expert handlers of the telephone.

If anything, the number of people you will speak to is an underestimation. You will be fortunate if you are not passed on two or three times. You will receive a 'hello' greeting from most of the staff, which doesn't help the conversation along at all. You will hold on for considerable periods, because you have been requested to hold on, and in the end you will wonder whether the operator has passed away.

If you telephone a retail store, you will either not get

through to the department at all or, when you do get through to the department, you will have to beg someone to sell you something.

You will agree, after testing this out, that there is a lot of profit to be made via the intelligent use of the telephone – and that a case has been made for the training of all staff who handle the telephone – but what about us? Do we sometimes fall by the wayside? Are we ever self-critical?

We must always remember that everyone in industry who speaks on the telephone, sells. The techniques taught in this book, learned from a lifetime of selling, therefore apply to everyone in industry, but most of all to those who live by being effective communicators – the salespeople.

CHAPTER 3

The Telephone Sales Presentation

If you have ever had to ask your bank for a large overdraft, then you will remember how carefully you laid your plans, and how you rehearsed your appeal over and over again. Remember the way you decided to build his confidence in you by quickly telling him of your promotion? Do you recollect the way you explained the many assets of the house you wanted to buy? Highly praised by the surveyor, a bargain compared to others in the vicinity, what a wonderful state of repair it was in, how it would save you money on fares to the office, its beautiful surroundings . . .

Whether you believed it or not, that was selling and, in fact, you were making a well-thought-out sales presentation because you didn't want to leave anything to chance.

If you have ever had to make an important speech, you will remember the elation you felt on receiving the request, followed by despair as you contemplated the enormity of the task. But you thought and thought around the subject, then you wrote out the speech in full, didn't you?

Tried to remember it, and failed. Then you edited the speech, got the gist of it, and found that brief notes helped you to remember the flow of scintillating, humorous, gripping, vital sentences. You rehearsed right up to the day of the speech. You mouthed the words on your way to work, and you mouthed them again on the way home.

That is exactly what most sensible people do when preparing a speech, and what most sensible salespeople do when preparing a presentation to sell on the telephone.

Yet some sales staff believe that they have no need for a prepared presentation, although those same people who believe they can sell off the cuff even rehearse the excuses they are going to make to their partners when they stay out late.

At our sales training courses, a full session is devoted to the phenomenon of men and women who daily use a sales sequence in their private lives, but do not believe it is necessary to master a sales presentation for sales interviews.

There is logic behind the sales sequence. If there is one best way to present a case, why use a string of words which add up to second best?

It has sometimes been said that selling begins when the buyer says 'No'. This, of course, is now known to be nonsense. The art of salesmanship is to employ words so skilfully that the big 'No' in the buyer's mind at the commencement of the sale diminishes into the little 'no' of an answerable objection, and then disappears altogether.

The weak salesperson – or even the strong salesperson with the poor sales sequence – often does not get past the first 'NO'. If he does, he has to fight a very hard battle to retrieve his cause.

The good sales presentation, therefore, can be the greatest of all problem solvers for telephone sales staff, because it will hold a buyer's interest and answer many of his objections without his having to voice them.

IT'S TOUGH

It is harder to sell a six-inch double column of space in a magazine by telephone than it would be if face-to-face with the buyer. It is more difficult to persuade a prospect to buy insurance over the telephone than when you make eye contact at an interview. It is tougher to sell a new range of products to a grocer over the telephone than it is for the salesperson making a regular visit. That is why the telephone salesperson must have a really tough streak if he is to stay with his job. Like a cold canvassing salesperson who works shop after shop or house after house, he has to take so many *no's* to obtain that *yes*. There is nothing unusual in this to a speciality salesperson, but other salespeople using the telephone to increase sales have to learn it the hard way. The well-thought-out sales sequence will increase the *yes's*, and decrease the *no's*.

Telephone selling is also tough because all of the appeal is aural. The majority of people are bad listeners, and buyers who are not eager to make a purchase, or prospects interrupted by the call during their routine work have *cottonwool eardrums*. They do not concentrate on what is being explained to them, and the salesperson cannot command their immediate interest by the use of visual aids. The buyer cannot see the brightness of the salesperson's eyes, the enthusiasm of her bearing or be influenced by her winning personality. Neither can the telephone salesperson involve the buyer's senses of smell, touch, taste or sight.

She is not able to say, 'Doesn't this perfume smell wonderful?' or 'Just feel the smoothness of the cloth,' or 'This taste is unique, isn't it?' or 'Look at the photograph of this burned factory.'

The challenge to the telephone salesperson is to overcome these obstacles inherent in this form of communication and build a sales presentation which will command a hearing. It must be designed to make the buyer agree, approve and act.

GOLDEN WORDS

During the first session on the second day of our telephone sales training course the instructor begins by saying, 'You live by the words you use . . .'

Sales staff selling person-to-person are assisted by brochures, drawings, letters, samples, or demonstration models, but the telephone salesperson depends solely on the *words she uses*. She must, therefore, polish every word, every sentence until he is positive that they have the right balance to tip the scales in her favour.

She must not use indecisive words such as:

possibly
maybe
I think
could be

She must try to use one word instead of two or more. Instead of: Use:

Instead of:	Use:
in as much as	*since*
with a view to	*to*
for that reason	*so*
on a basis of	*by*
according to our records	*we find*

check our records	*check*
a large number of	*many*
along the lines of	*like*
during the time that	*while*
in consideration of	*considering*
in view of the fact that	*because*
in the very near future	*soon*
without making any noise	*noiselessly*

Also, more expressive, descriptive words should be used:

Instead of:	Use:
it is a fine design	*it is an exquisite design*
you will get good results	*you will get excellent results*
it has a bright finish	*it has a glowing finish*
it will remove odours	*it will banish odours*
we are sorry you are dissatisfied	*your frank comments are appreciated*

The telephone salesperson can only use a few hundred words to complete a sales story. Face-to-face he could be using two to four thousand words. This is another reason why every word must have punch, power, and appeal.

PRE-PLANNING

Analysis by self-questioning is essential if the presentation is to have depth and appeal.

QUESTION 1
Have I complete product knowledge?
Can your company deliver from stock? If not, what is the time lag? Are all colours in stock? Can specials be supplied? What are the technical advantages of your product? What is the technical advantage claimed by your competitors? What service do you offer? Does your company service equipment through dealers or direct? What is the service time lag? Is there a charge for installation? Are you conversant with all forms of packaging? What credit terms are offered? Are you up-to-date with all advertising plans, sales promotion schemes, merchandising? Do you understand the small print on the agreements or policies? . . .

QUESTION 2
What is the general market for my products?
This can readily be answered in the consumer field (not forgetting canteens, hospitals, clubs, etc.) but if you are selling capital equipment or a specialised service, then more research may be necessary. For example:

Selling advertising space
Space sales staff sell mainly through advertising agents, but there are other fields worth investigating. Space could be sold direct to the smaller manufacturer, retailer or dealer who may not have an agent.

Selling insurance
Everyone needs insurance, pensions, etc. and most of the likely prospects are contacted regularly by insurance salespeople. Very few insurance salespeople call on retail shops, however. Would that be a market?

Publicans are more receptive to salespeople than

managing directors yet they, again, are rarely contacted by insurance salespeople unless they have made an enquiry. Also, publicans can give leads for further business.

What other outlets are there?

Selling office equipment
The larger offices and factories obviously have the greatest buying potential, but there are other outlets which the telephone sales staff could investigate. Restaurant proprietors buy PCs, but are seldom sold them. Small hotel owners are rarely contacted. Ex-secretaries who offer a word processing service can also be contacted. They may update their PCs regularly.

These examples could be multiplied many times and applied to every industry. Extra outlets can be discovered and covered quickly by the telephone sales staff.

QUESTION 3
Why should anyone buy my products?
The kernel of the sales presentation must stress the benefits to the buyer. The salesperson can only unearth these benefits if she is aware of the main reasons why her prospect or customer needs he service or products.

Turning needs into wants
Many a prospect may need your product, but he may not want it, and the majority of buyers satisfy their wants rather than their *needs*.

He may *need* insurance, but *want* an extra holiday. The house may *need* rewiring, but she *wants* a cashmere suit.

He may *need* a computer, but he *wants* a new head office built in rural surroundings.

He *needs* extra stock, but he *wants* cash in the bank.

He *needs* a series of advertisements, but he *wants* to economise.

What will be the decision of those buyers if their mind is not influenced by a salesperson? They will decide on their *wants*.

The insurance salesperson must convince her prospect that for the sake of his family he should forgo that extra holiday and give his wife and children immediate protection in the event of his death.

The electrical contractor will point out to the householder the great risk she is running of fire, so that she will *want* to have her house rewired before buying the cashmere suit.

The managing director must be persuaded that there would be little sense in a head office in the country if her business efficiency suffered. The salesperson must convince the managing director to want the computer more than the country surroundings.

The salesperson selling consumer durables must stress to the buyer the risk he is running in losing business to his competitors when he runs down stock, and that the stocks will bring him a greater return than will be received from bank deposits.

The advertiser must be made to realise that to insert only one advertisement is false economy.

The sales presentation must be so strong that the *need* for the product or service will be turned into the greatest possible *want,* and so overcome the urge of a buyer to spend money in other directions.

STEPS TO THE ORDER

There must be a logical sequence to every sales presentation. The first recorded sales story (the euphemism 'sales presentation' came later) was written by a salesman employed by the National Cash Register Company. Later it became the basis of the sequence used by all NCR salesmen. The AIDA formula became a by-word in selling and, since then, hardly a book on salesmanship has failed to mention AIDA, a sales presentation based on these steps:

Attention
Interest
Desire
Action

This sequence was right, but the very wordy sales story built around it failed because it was meant to be learned verbatim and spoken parrotwise. Men, however, are not parrots.

During the early '30's, we changed the AIDA formula to embrace additional steps, but made it easier to learn because the salesperson had only to memorise a few sentences. The salesperson, or sales trainer, would write the sequence in full, underlining the lead sentences to each step. Only lead sentences had to be remembered, because each held the key to the step which followed. That step could be elaborated by the salesperson by words of his own choosing. The sentences act as reminders to a salesperson to keep to a sequence, but in his own words.

This combined the best of both worlds – the ability to use a complete presentation while, at the same time, expressing one's own personality. Since then, many thousands of salespeople have used the *Tack Selling Sentence* technique successfully. It is just as simple to use with the shortened telephone selling sequence.

The sequence for person-to-person selling is now:
1. Contact and Approach
2. Creation of Interest
3. Confidence-building
4. Communicating of Benefits of Product/Service
5. Creation of Desire
6. Clarifying Difference (or Objective)
7. Commitment for Customer

Main selling and reminder sentences are used for each step, but when covering service or benefits, four or eight main sentences are used, product benefits being the focal point of the presentation.

Every single benefit has to be stressed. A salesman must, therefore, find every reason why the prospect should buy, and these reasons are expressed as *Benefits*.

The Telephone Sequence
The telephone salesperson will adopt a procedure similar to that of the person-to-person salesman but with a difference. Although she will still write the presentation in full, she will only look for one main benefit, and one subsidiary benefit. There is no time in telephone selling to build benefit on benefit.

A telephone salesperson selling a range of goods, beauty products, for example, will book orders for the majority of her standard creams and lotions, but build her presentation on the one line that is being specially promoted. The benefits of this special product will be stressed – *the uniquely designed bottle, the new ingredient, the advertising campaign*, etc.

There are other changes in the sequence that the telephone salesperson must make. *Creating Interest* can no longer be a separate step, and neither can *Confidence-building*. *Contact and Approach* must create immediate interest, while confidence-building can be used at the most appropriate time during the presentation.

To a salesperson who is extremely well known to his customer, confidence-building need only be a reminder of the wide publicity the new product is receiving, or the way the old product has steadily increased sales because of the sales promotional plans. If a salesperson is unknown to the prospect, then he will have to introduce confidence building a little earlier – 'You have probably heard of us, our Company were the originators of . . .' or '. . . have just linked up with . . .'

The telephone salesperson's logical sequence, therefore, will be:

Approach and Interest
Main Benefit
Subsidiary Benefit
Close

} Create Confidence

Although, in this chapter, the direct sales presentation is being covered, now is the time to explain that, when seeking an interview, a sequence has again to be changed.

The sequence for obtaining an interview is:

Contact and Approach
Main Benefit
Benefit of Personal Interview
Appointment Close

Whether you are selling a service, a range of goods or

capital equipment, whether you sell insurance or advertising signs, whether you sell space or whether you only use the telephone to obtain appointments, always remember that the pre-planning of a sales presentation is the sure way to success.

CONTACT AND APPROACH

Put yourself in the shoes of your buyer or prospect, for example the owner of a grocery shop, an office manager or a managing director. People with no time to spare during the day, but having priorities to enable them to use their time effectively.

The salesperson calling upon a retailer busily serving a customer, stands aside and waits until the retailer finishes the transaction. That retailer, however, is determined to check his stock as soon as his customer leaves. The arrival of the salesperson faces him with two alternatives: he can dismiss the salesperson with a 'Sorry, I'm busy', or he can see him and put off stock-taking.

How the salesperson acts during the first few seconds after the retailer's customer has left the shop will determine whether or not he is allowed to stay and sell.

The office manager spends his time e-mailing, answering correspondence, attending meetings, inter-viewing applicants for positions, completing forms, etc. He, therefore, will also have little free time except during meal breaks.

The managing director, if she is efficient, will have a timetable worked out for her by her PA to which she will adhere – a time for meetings, a time for problem-solving, a time for visiting different locations.

So, now you have a picture of three busy people – a retailer, an office manager, and a managing director – into whose shoes you are going to step.

How would you react if your task of the moment was interrupted by an unexpected telephone call?

If you were the retailer, how would feel when your customer is leaving, the salesman is trying to persuade you to see him, the stock needs checking, and a supplier telephones to discuss a new promotional effort?

You are now the office manager. The managing director has just been tearing strips off you for staff slackness in the office and, as he is about to leave, the telephone rings and someone wants to sell you a computer.

Now, as a managing director you are worrying about the cash flow, concerned at falling sales, dictating letters and memoranda to the accountant and the sales manager. The telephone rings – it is a salesperson wanting to increase your insurances.

All executives, shop owners, doctors, or dentists are faced with this problem of how to allocate their time, and they never allow for the unexpected telephone call. No director will tell his PA to leave free a few minutes in every hour to accept telephone calls from strangers, or comparative strangers.

Whatever time of the day you telephone, your customer or prospect will be busy. A doctor will be about to see a patient, a dentist perhaps talking to her mechanic, a space buyer involved in data analysis . . .

It is only by creating an interesting and compelling approach that you will encourage a prospect or buyer to put aside what he is doing and listen.

You have a choice of many alternatives when

considering your approach. It could be based on one of the following:

a fact
a question
something topical
something to arouse curiosity
a reference from a friend or business associate
advertising
a TV campaign
an exhibition
a letter written previously
a gift
caution
a service
a promotional campaign
a bargain offer

Here are some examples of various approaches:

QUESTION APPROACH	Good morning, is that Mr. Brown?'
	'Yes.'
Repeat name	'Mr. Brown, this is Tom Smith of the Decorative Flower Company. Do you find that a high proportion of women make bookings for your family holidays?'
	'Yes, that's true.'
	'Mr. Brown, then a bowl of our gorgeous flowers placed in your window would attract attention.

They are real window stoppers . . .'

REFERENCE APPROACH	'Mr. White?' 'Yes.'
Repeat name, and make courtesy request	'Mr. White, can you spare me a few moments?' 'Yes.' 'This is Tom Smith of Direct Supplies Ltd. Recently we were able to make drastic reductions in the cost of printer cartridges for your friend Ms. Lever of Lever & Jenkins. She told me she felt sure you would want to make similar Savings and suggested that I telephone you . . .'
CAUTION APPROACH	'Mr. Green?' 'Yes.'
Repeat name	'Mr. Green, this is Pat Smith of Causeway Garages. It's just ten months since you purchased your car from us. When you called in for a service the other day, our attendant noticed that the treads on your tyres were wearing. You know, Mr. Green, Sometimes we

only discover a tyre problem when it's too late.

BARGAIN APPROACH	'Ms. Blue?' 'Yes.'
Repeat name	'Ms. Blue, this is Toyah Smith of Apex Toiletries. My reason for calling you is that new price schedules are coming into effect on the first. As an old and loyal customer, I wanted to give you the special opportunity of placing an order now for your future requirements . . .

Study the list of suggested approaches and attempt to ally each one of them to your product or service. This will prove the practicability of creating novel but strong approaches.

After carrying out these exercises you will decide on the main appeal of your product or service. You will change the approach, at intervals, because selling is not static. Your company may launch a new advertising campaign or a new product. Trial and error may prove to you that the factual approach is better than an advertising approach. You will, however, always keep to an approach that immediately arouses interest, irrespective of how tired you may become of using it. If it works, it's right.

THE MAIN AND SUBSIDIARY BENEFITS

If you are selling a house, does your client buy it from you because of the depth of its foundation, the specially glazed bricks facing the outside walls, or the solidity of its structure? Or does he buy it because of the pride he will feel in his new home, future capital appreciation, the warmth of the central heating, and the easy-work kitchen?

If you are selling a new line in fresh soups, does the caterer buy from you because of the freshness of the vegetables used, the modern conversion plant or the new airtight packaging, or because he believes that the new soups will please his customers and increase his margin of profit?

Why do People Buy?
People buy for personal benefit, to satisfy a human need. The main consideration of a space buyer contemplating advertising in a magazine is: will it bring in enough enquiries to make the advertisement profitable? A secondary benefit might be pride in the impact the advertisement will make on his customers. A third benefit, the praise he may receive from his managing director for the success of the campaign.

If a telephone salesperson selling space were trying to close the order with that buyer she would, therefore, make her main benefit *profit*, and her secondary benefit *satisfaction* of pride or *to gain praise*.

Parents buy for the good health or amusement of their children; managing directors sometimes buy to increase their own ego.

Company reports published in newspapers are often

not intended to inform so much as to raise the status of the chairman or managing director in the eyes of *the City*. A retailer could buy because of fear – fear that if he did not become an internet supplier, a competitor might get in first and take away some of his business.

In the industrial world, the main buying reason is nearly always financial gain or financial saving, but there is a wide variety of subsidiary reasons. In telephone selling we can only give the main benefit and one *subsidiary* benefit.

The following buying motivators are not all-embracing, but they will cover 80-90% of buying reasons:

> financial gain
> financial saving
> to appease caution
> to satisfy pride
> to avoid effort
> comfort
> sentiment
> pleasure
> health
> to satisfy hunger
> utility value
> envy
> love
> to obtain security
> to obtain more leisure
> to satisfy ego
> to protect family
> to attract opposite sex
> to gain popularity
> to gain praise
> safety

to possess beautiful objects
to impress others.

Product Analysis

The next step in building your sales presentation is company service and product analysis.

Sometimes it is essential to prove a need first, but a need must always be turned into a want.

Before this objective can be reached, we must define the main reasons for the prospect or customer wanting a product or service. This want will stem from the benefits which he will derive from the product, reinforced by the confidence he has in the company and its ability to maintain quality, promises of delivery etc.

First, then, must come company analysis:
Is the company the leader in its field?
When was it established?
What are its future plans?
Where are its locations? (Parochialism still exists.)
How many staff members are engaged in research?
Who is head of the research division? What is her
    background?
Is the managing director known in any sphere other
    than his own?

Next must come product or service analysis:
Is it new?
How long has it been on the market?
Is it derived from a successful predecessor?
Why is it ahead of competitors' products?
How is it constructed?
Why is it less expensive?
Why is it more expensive?
Has it prestige value?

Is it better packaged?
Is it covered by a long-term guarantee?
Is the brand widely known?
Does it hold the greater share of the market?
Is demand increasing?
Can quick service be carried out?
Can it be adapted specially for a customer?
Is it a novelty?
Will it sell all the year round?

The product analysis must be in-depth, and only when all the benefits are listed can the telephone salesperson begin to work out her own presentation. This is how one salesperson set about the task.

Case Study
A telephone salesperson selling a ventilating system to an office manager – needing a unit for his office – lists product facts, benefits and buying reasons:

Silent in operation.	Meeting occupational health and safety requirements because noise affects health – *health benefits*.
Stops condensation.	Decoration needed at less frequent intervals – *saves money*.
Slimline outline.	As unit is visible outside the building – *satisfies pride*.
Unit extracts at 41,000 cfh.	Better atmosphere will result in increased output of staff – *profit*.
Draught-free.	Desks can be placed near

	windows. Better use of office space – *saves money*.
Unit ventilates at 43,000 cfh.	Less risk of infection – *fear*. Less absenteeism – *saves money*.
Extracts smoke.	Smoke discolours decorations and impregnates furnishings – *saves money*.
Extracts odours.	Working in odour-free atmosphere – *gives pleasure*.
Gives exact air changes required.	*Utility value*.
Metal non-corrosive.	Long life, easy maintenance – *saves money*.
Protective grilles.	Less risk of accident – *security*.
Three-year guarantee.	*Satisfaction of caution*.

This analysis shows there are five buying reasons for saving money and one each for *profit, pride, fear, pleasure, caution, utility value, security, health*.

Although, in this example, there are five *saving money* buying reasons, this does not necessarily mean that when analysing products, the main benefit must always be based on the majority of buying reasons shown by analysis. However, in this case study, the salesperson decides to concentrate on *saving money* as the main benefit which must lead to increased profitability.

Which means that
The salesperson knows that his prospects are not really interested in technicalities, but only in the benefits they derive from them. He therefore reminds himself that he must always express benefits in terms of buyers' interests.

So that he never forgets this fact during a presentation, he uses three link words:

which means that

This is how he would use the link words:

'It is silent in operation, Ms. Brown, *which means that* the health of your staff will not be affected by noise.'

'It stops condensation, Mr. Smith, *which means that* you will save money by decorating less frequently.'

'Ms. White, the metal is non-corrosive, *which means that* the Nu-aire will have a long life, the maintenance is easy and it will always keep its new look.'

Always remember the words *which means that.*

The salesperson now concentrates on building the lead-in sentences regarding the:

main and subsidiary benefits.

Having made the decision to concentrate on saving money and increasing profit, he looks again at the twelve features of his unit and concludes that he will have to stress the benefits of working in a clean, fresh atmosphere. Finally, he puts together the sentence:

You can turn an eight-hour day into an eight-hour working day.

That is the sentence he will memorise and on which he will build his step, by noting points to remember:

*staff work better in a clean atmosphere
*no decline in productivity in the afternoon due to heavy atmosphere.

Next, he concentrates on the subsidiary step, and he creates the sentence:

Fatigue is more a matter of atmosphere than of hours.

This sentence he also memorises, and again notes points to remember:

*tiredness makes staff susceptible to colds and flu
*tiredness causes irritability, quarrels, less productivity
*tiredness causes headaches.

To recap, the main sentence is:
You can turn an eight-hour day into an eight-hour working day,
and the subsidiary sentence is:
Fatigue is more a matter of atmosphere than of hours.
These will be the sentences to be memorised, and expanded upon, according to a prospect's needs. However, there is still more work to be done before the presentation can be finalised.

'YES' RESPONSES

Making statements, however good they may be, is not good salesmanship.
Why?
Because we do not know:

(a) if the prospect has heard us
(b) if he has understood us
(c) if he agrees with us.

We, therefore, have to adopt a technique of making positive statements, and asking positive questions which will evoke 'yes' responses. When we have our prospect's agreement, we know that we can continue with our presentation.

The telephone salesperson will, therefore, prepare a number of questions to which she is certain of getting a 'yes' response.

'Ms. Brown, the number of air changes required in an office varies from two to four. You would like to have instant control of those air changes, wouldn't you?'

'Yes.'

'One popular feature of our units is the variable control. At full speed, you will remove 41,000 cubic feet of air per hour, *which means that* you will still have perfect conditions even when the fan is operating against a head wind. Ms. Brown, at the moment, when you want to ventilate the office, you have to open the windows, is that right?'

'Yes.'

'And Ms. Brown, when the window is open, isn't it draughty for the staff working at desks near the window?'

'Yes, we have had complaints.'

'Well, there will be no draughts when our unit is installed, *which means that* you will be able to place desks right alongside the windows if necessary. You would like to make use of that extra floorspace, wouldn't you?'

'Yes, it would help.'

'By the way, Ms. Brown, I am sure you will agree that *fatigue is often more a matter of atmosphere than of hours.* That is why staff tend to ease off during the afternoon. We all feel drowsy in a stuffy atmosphere, don't we?'

'Yes, I suppose we do.'

'The unit will circulate the air when necessary, extract

air, or bring air in. It will prove its worth during the winter and the summer, because research has shown that good air conditioning is one of the sure ways of cutting down absenteeism, *which means that* you won't be spending money paying wages to staff who are ill in bed with flu and colds.'

In giving these examples of 'yes' responses, the customer's agreement has been obtained after each question. This does not always happen. She could raise an objection – but objections will be dealt with in a later chapter. However, when the objection is answered, the telephone salesperson must obtain the 'yes' response, to be sure that the prospect is satisfied. This presentation is based on the day-to-day work of a salesperson in this field, telephoning in response to an enquiry, the prospect having had all the relevant data regarding size, price, and fixing.

Here are the kinds of questions which can be asked by salespeople working in other spheres:

- 'You do agree that advertising on the packet is good advertising, don't you, Mr. Smith?'
- 'You would like to increase your profit margin, wouldn't you, Mr. White?'
- 'If you could cut costs by five per cent right away, you would want to start immediately, wouldn't you?'
- 'Ms. Brown, you wouldn't like to take any risks for one day longer than you need, so I am sure you would like to be covered right away, wouldn't you?'
- 'You do risk losing custom when you are out of stock, don't you?'
- 'A series of advertisements would bring far better results against cost, I am sure you agree with that, Ms. Johnson . . .'

To Remind You

When building a presentation:

1. Use golden words – expressive words.
2. Know your product – know your market.
3. Keep to the sequence:
   Contact and Approach ⎫
   Main Benefit   ⎬ Create Confidence
   Subsidiary Benefit   ⎪
   Close   ⎭
4. Base the approach on a compelling reason for the buyer to listen to you.
5. Remember to turn needs into *wants*.
6. Base benefits on buying reasons.
7. Analyse products and services to find buying reasons and benefits.
8. Create and memorise selling sentences to remind you of the complete step . . . *which means that* you will be able to move smoothly into the close.

OBTAINING COMMITMENT
OR CLOSING THE SALE

Often a play or musical fails on opening in a London theatre after a provincial run. Then the excuses flow from the producer, director, actors and actresses: 'We opened at the wrong time' – 'The weather was against us' – 'The critics panned us unfairly' – 'We were affected by the strike . . .'

These excuses make no allowance for the fact that other shows manage to carry on in spite of these difficulties.

When a production fails the reason can usually be traced to mistakes in judgement: the playwright would not accept changes – others involved refused to accept criticism – the actors and actresses were badly cast, etc. Problems during the provincial run were waived aside as being of no consequence – with everyone saying 'It will be all right on the night!' But the show was doomed to failure from the beginning. Would the playwright ever admit this? Would the actor agree that he was inaudible to the back row? Would the producer believe that the play, which had a special message, couldn't find an audience who wanted to listen to that message?

The failure was not due to any sudden change in the weather, or a strike, or even because the critics panned it. Many shows have succeeded despite such criticism. The play failed way back.

It is very similar to a sale. Sales are never lost at the last moment. The mistakes are made much earlier. All telephone salespeople should write on a card:

I do not lose orders because of my weak closing techniques.
I lose orders because my presentation is not good enough.

That is the first lesson to be learned if more orders are to be obtained. The old selling axiom that *a good sale closes itself* is still true. Sometimes, however, a buyer, even although he is well sold, is still hesitant, and there are many ways of nudging the buyer into saying, 'I'll go ahead.'

What is meant by the *professional* salesperson is a question I am often asked. Is a man of fifty, after thirty years on the road, a truly professional salesman, while the man with only three years' experience is an amateur?

Not at all. Some amateurs are old-time salespeople

who believe that they are fully experienced because of the time they have spent facing customers. How about the dynamic young man? The quick-witted, fast talker – he could also be an amateur, although he is sure that he is a professional.

The professional salesperson:

(a) learns from experience. She doesn't believe that by the act of calling on customers she is necessarily gaining experience in salesmanship. She knows that experience comes from analysing the calls, pinpointing mistakes, and assessing the need for change.

(b) She is interested in her work and is always eager to improve her selling skills. She knows that only a genius can break fundamental rules in salesmanship or sport, and succeed. She also knows there are not many geniuses about.

Unfortunately, amateur salespeople believe they are endowed with special qualities, and that they can break the rules or even not bother to learn the rules, and still succeed.

The telephone salesperson must also learn the fundamentals of telephone selling and become truly professional by applying them.

Here are some basic rules for closing orders:

1. There must be no attempt to get a commitment from the customer until you are certain that your prospect understands your proposition. Orders closed too quickly lead to cancellations. The exception is when a prospect understands her requirements, and expresses her willingness to buy. For example, she might say, 'I know all about it and have been considering the idea for some time. I suppose I should have made up my

mind . . .' That prospect knows what she wants, and the salesperson must close the order.

2. You must always ask for the order, but if you fail, you must leave the door open so that your next call will be welcome. On making your second call, be positive and assume that the decision is in your favour. Never ask, 'Have you made up your mind?' Take up a point from the previous call and continue from that point:

> 'Mr. Brown, when I spoke to you yesterday you were concerned that our prices were more expensive than our main competitor. Well, Mr. Brown, I have given this serious thought. They could probably reduce their prices even further. The fact that we are unable to do so proves to you not only the quality of our product, but its salability. After all, our products have been succeeding for over twenty years . . .'

3. When the order is closed the salesperson must ring off quickly, after a sentence to cement confidence:

> 'I'll telephone you again when it is delivered.'
> 'I'll make sure it is delivered on time.'
> 'You will be delighted when it is installed.'

4. When selling consumer goods, the salesperson will close quickly on each line as it is offered.

5. Assume that the order is yours from the very first words of the approach. This positiveness on your part will come through over the telephone early in the presentation. Use such explicit statements as:

> 'You can telephone me personally if ever you require service.'
> 'You will like the chair because of its appearance, but most of all because of its comfort when you sit down in the evenings.'

'Your advertisement will have tremendous appeal and will get a sure response . . .'

6. *Buying Signals*

The telephone salesperson must be brief and must always close if she receives a buying signal when the presentation is nearing its conclusion. The prospect may say:

'Do you find they are selling well?'
'Can you deliver quickly?'
'What did you say the measurements are?'
'Will it help to avoid . . .'
'You did say I should have exclusive rights for a month?'
'What are your credit terms?'
'Will I have any problem in obtaining spares?'

These are definite buying signals. Listen to them. They prove that the prospect is sold and it is only a question of asking for the order.

HOW TO ASK FOR COMMITMENT

The direct request can be made:
'May I place the order for you?'
'Will you give me an order number?'

You might win, but you might precipitate the clicking of the receiver as it is set down. The prospect's 'NO' is so final.

The Alternative Close

It is far better to offer the prospect alternatives:
– 'Would you prefer to order one month's supply or

two months' supply with the special discount?'
- 'It could be installed in the window facing south or the one facing east. Which is your preference?'
- 'Would you prefer our cleaning staff to arrive early in the morning or after you have closed in the evenings?'

If any of these alternatives generates an indecisive reply, the salesperson has still not lost the order, or command of the situation. He can continue selling.

Research has shown that 74% of all telephone salespeople use the *alternative* as a closing aid. Often, however, the *alternative close* is linked with other methods of finalising the presentation. These can be closes within their own right, but when the buyer needs an extra nudge, use the *alternative close*.

These are proven closing techniques:

Concession Close

When selling consumer goods, special promotions and concessions are usually part of the sales presentation. There are occasions when a salesperson is allowed to grant a concession which is not applicable to all of her customers; extra discount, longer credit, special deliveries, thirteen for twelve, a free service, a refund guarantee . . .'

Many telephone salespeople give the concession at the approach, but this is wrong. The rule is: *sell as if you did not have the concession*. The order might close easily and you have no need to give away some of your company's profits. It is when the order is proving difficult to close that the concession can have real weight.

The Summary Close

In telephone selling, the presentation is so short that the

majority of prospects will retain the main points in their mind, but there is always the buyer who only half-listens and even gives 'yes' responses automatically.

For those buyers, the telephone salesperson summarises the main features and benefits of his product and then asks for the order.

The *summary close* is sometimes called the *reminder close*.

The Cautionary Close

This is used by salespeople selling fire extinguishers, burglar alarms, safes, insurance, and many other products and services. The telephone salesperson selling consumer or consumer durables can sometimes use it when (a) the customer is afraid of running out of stock during a busy time, or (b) a competitor will obtain preferential support.

Used judiciously, the *cautionary close* can activate the prospect who hesitates to place an order for capital equipment, or to stock a new line.

The Verbal Proof Story Close

This close is similar to the *reference approach*. It is a confidence-builder, and can prove most helpful when selling to a timid buyer.

The telephone salesperson concludes his presentation with a success story. A telephone salesperson selling advertising space to the owner of a TV and radio store might say:

'Ms. Brown, you do know Pickles of Wrexton, don't you . . .?'
'Yes, they are well known in the trade.'
'So are you, Ms. Brown, but I think it will interest you to hear that Mr. Pickles was very hesitant about taking

space in our magazine. Like you, he thought the local press would be better for him. Also, he wanted to cut down on his advertising expenditure, not increase it. But he decided to take a full page, and the response was so good that he has now booked a whole series. You would find the same would happen to you, Ms. Brown . . .'

The rule applying to the *verbal proof story* is that it must be true, and applicable, and relating to a business away from the locality in which the prospect is situated.

Closing on a Minor Point
This is part *assumption* and part *alternative close*. The telephone salesperson will say:

'You do agree, Mr. Brown, that you prefer a remote control with the unit, don't you?'
'Mr. Smith, we deliver Thursday. Would that be all right for you?'
'As it is a present, Ms. Jones, would you like it specially gift-wrapped?'

The telephone salesperson must assume that if the prospect agrees on the *minor point*, she is ready to place the order.

The Isolation Close
The telephone salesperson separates the one point that is holding up the order. He ignores irrelevant differences and says firmly:

'Ms. Brown, the single point which makes you hesitate is that you believe that our minimum order is too large for you. Let me put this in its right perspective: I should be letting you down if I supplied you with less than our minimum, because you would not be able to satisfy the demand, and we couldn't deliver a fresh supply to you in time . . .'

'All that separates us, Mr. Jones, is that you need extended credit facilities. This is what we can do to help you . . .'

OBTAIN THAT COMMITMENT

It is always fear which stops prospects from buying – fear of making a mistake, fear of reprimand from higher authority, fear of spending too much money, fear of loss of security, fear of what his wife or her husband will say, fear of over-stocking, fear of being talked into an order etc.

You must calm their fears by closing in a positive manner. Until the sale is closed, the salesperson is a conversationalist. Only when the order is finalised is he a salesman.

CHAPTER 4

Your Voice Is Your Selling Personality

Although the telephone salesperson has the disadvantage of being unable to use visual aids, she has the advantage of not being in a position to distract a buyer. During face-to-face selling, mannerisms can be sales losers. A salesperson may pick a spot on his face, jingle his keys, play with a pen, or do an off-and-on act with his glasses. If he has a cold, he may sneeze and blow his nose every few seconds. The telephone salesperson can indulge his mannerisms without necessarily impairing his sales presentation. He knows that he sells by the words he uses and the personality of his voice.

A lacklustre voice can have the same effect on a buyer as a salesperson's lethargic expression when selling face-to-face. For your presentation to be 100% effective, for your listener to warm to you over the telephone, and, more important, to hear and understand every word of your sales sequence, you must have a good telephone voice.

But that is the problem. We all think we have a good voice – it is a part of us, the way we are made . . .

Or is it? Unless there is some deformity, everyone has similar vocal chords, diaphragm, and tongue. We are not born with round shoulders; we develop them through having bad posture. We are not born without the ability to smile; some people smile more than others as they mature. So it is with the voice. Speaking is an imitative faculty. Our speech, generally, is a result of birthplace, upbringing, and association with others. By the time we reach our twenties, the voice we use is definitive. If, however, we have the determination, we can improve it in the same way as we can straighten our backs.

It has so often been said that you cannot change people. The comment may be made in reference to someone's meanness, selfishness, hardness or lack of common sense. In such cases, people rarely do change as they live out their lives. Others may suffer from psychological problems – irrational fears, timidity, arrogance or a propensity to lie. Psychiatrists can sometimes eradicate these traits.

Sales training does not set out to change people, but to increase their natural attributes. Anyone unhappy about the sound of her voice or diction can, by effort and determination, put matters right.

In business we are expected to speak acceptably to our customers, but this is vital if you are a telephone salesperson. Always remember the voice – that wonderful instrument you use when shaping and making words.

VOICE PROJECTION

Voice projection is based on good breathing. Good breathing means correct breathing. Correct breathing means controlled breathing, or taking in the right amount of breath at the right place, and using it in order to give the right emotive power which makes for voice quality.

When we don't control our breathing properly, we become breathless, which results in irregular rhythm and poor voice quality. Most people, when attempting to put more power in their voice, concentrate on their vocal chords. Unfortunately, this only causes tension in the muscles surrounding the vocal chords, resulting in a dry wheezy tone of voice. To improve your voice quality, you must concentrate instead on your lungs. You will then have taken your first step towards diaphragmatic breathing.

When we sell, either face-to-face or over the telephone, we have to maintain voice power and voice quality to communicate effectively. This can only be brought about by correct breathing.

Test 1

Place the palm of your hand firmly on that V-shape in the breastbone, just below the rib. You can now feel the diaphragm working gently. Next, imagine that you have just raced round the block and you are puffing hard. Start puffing. Now you can feel the diaphragm working really hard.

This is what is happening: as you inhale, your lungs expand, pushing the elastic diaphragm down and out. As you exhale, the diaphragm goes in and up, resulting in more rapid propulsion of the outgoing air passing over the vocal chords.

When speaking, you inhale more rapidly and exhale more slowly. This enables you to conserve your breath to make words and sentences.

Test 2

Imagine that you have just enjoyed a wonderful meal prepared by a cordon bleu chef, with specially selected vintage wines; you have been the guest of honour and your virtues have been extolled. Having made your speech, and received warm and generous applause, you sit back in your chair feeling that all is well with the world.

You sigh. It is a deep sigh of repletion and content-
ment. Have you got the picture? Right, now sigh deeply.
Once more. How deeply you breathed! That sigh exercise is basically all that you need to know about breath
replenishment.

Test 3
Ideally, all breath should enter through the nostrils to
filter and warm it. However, this can sometimes be noisy
and jerky in its effect. For silence and efficiency, therefore,
breath may be taken in through a slightly open mouth.

Now breathe in through your mouth while it is only
slightly open. When you reach what you believe to be the
absolute limit of expansion of the diaphragm, take in a
little more breath – there will be more expansion. Then,
try once more. You will be surprised to discover that
there is nearly always some room left for expansion.
Conversely, when you think that you have emptied your
lungs of air, there is nearly always some breath left, and
some energy left in the diaphragm, to give the air that
extra propulsion. This should show you that, when
necessary, you have the ability to speak long sentences
without taking breath. In this manner, you may produce
a smooth vocal tone, without jerkiness.

EXERCISES

The following exercises will help you to gain effective
breath control:

Exercise 1
To ease throat muscular tension, sit in a chair and relax
your head and shoulders. First, allow your left shoulder,

and then your right shoulder to slump towards your chest, with your arms falling between your legs. Roll your head forward on to the chest and breathe deeply six times, saying to yourself; 'Let go – let go . . .' The word *let* as you breathe in, and *go* as you breathe out.

Exercise 2

Stand in front of a mirror and breathe in deeply and out slowly. The mirror will enable you to make certain that you are not lifting your shoulders. Most people lift their shoulders up as they breathe deeply, but this action does not help your breathing at all. As you breathe in, count to five, increasing this daily until you can reach eight. Count to ten as you start to breathe out, and increase this until you reach twenty or more. Repeat this exercise six times. You will not need to take such deep breaths when speaking normally, but this exercise will help you to develop your breath control.

Exercise 3

Mark off in a book several medium to long sentences, and read these sentences aloud in one breath.

Exercise 4

To maintain correct breathing, but to put a lilt in your voice, carry out the following exercise:

Sing part of a song, e.g., 'Land of Hope and Glory', or any popular song.

Sing the line three times, then stop. Say the words once more, but without taking breath, repeating the words in your normal speaking voice. This will help to make your voice mellow and melodious. You will find that after singing the refrain, you will not be able to drop into a flat, conversational style.

Exercise 5
For three minutes each morning, practise reading aloud from a book. Your rhythm will depend on your breathing. This will enable you to speak rythmically.

FORMING WORDS

'He's tongue-tied.' When we say that, we usually mean that someone doesn't communicate well. But speakers in every category are often tongue-tied in a different sense. They do not realise that the tongue is meant to move into position in order to establish sounds accurately. A flexible tongue must work in conjunction with a mobile jaw, to give clarity to the words we use. Few speakers open their mouths sufficiently, which results in an imperfect and muffled tone. You cannot speak effectively through half-closed lips.

Exercise 1
(a) Yawn. That's easy, isn't it? Yawn six times. This will help you to have a more mobile jaw.
(b) Repeat six times *you, why,* and *Yokohama,* exaggerating each word as you say it. Carry out this exercise morning and evening.

Exercise 2
(a) So that your tongue can become more mobile, place a finger in front of your mouth, about one inch away. Try to touch your finger with your tongue.
(b) Move your finger a little further away and try again.
(c) Keep your tongue straight, then try imitating a snake by flicking out your tongue. Try to reach your finger.
(d) Try to touch the tip of your nose with your tongue.

Repeat these exercises six times.

GOOD DICTION

Many a time you must have wondered if your hearing was impaired when listening to an after-dinner speaker. Only good manners prohibit you from shouting, 'I can't hear what you are saying'.

We now know that this lack of clarity can be due to many factors. It can happen, however, even when a speaker is shouting, because the outline of his words may be blurred.

This can be corrected by the better use of certain sounds – they are called consonants. Sounds such as P T D CH K L M N give greater emphasis and sharper authority to the words we use.

Here are some examples of poorly pronounced words:

Lazn'genlmn	instead of	ladies and gentlemen
awnjuice	instead of	orange juice
azamarrafac'	instead of	as a matter of fact

The *t*'s have disappeared, and also a *d* in the first example, and an *r* in the second.

Lazy pronunciation must be avoided at all costs by the telephone salesperson. Here are some more examples:

> baddle for battle
> liddle for little
> boddle for bottle
> fordy for forty
> kep' for kept
> cruss for crusts
> twen'y for twenty

Exercises
Use lazy pronunciation in front of a mirror and then correct yourself. You will be able to watch your mouth and notice how much more active your tongue is in the correct pronunciation.

THE VOWELS

The consonants are standard, but vowel sounds can change the type of speech we use. We all remember a, e, i, o, u, but, of course, there are many other vowel sounds as well. Effective vowel use is achieved by the elasticity of the lips. Without this flexibility, we are apt to say *terdye* instead of *today, feller* instead of *fellow,* and *ejicate* instead of *educate.*

Exercise 1
In front of a mirror, whisper a, e, i, o, u. Can you see your lips moving? Repeat a little louder, watching for the lip movements. Shout out the sounds. Now you can see your lips moving. Next, mouth the vowels without making a sound. Exaggerate the effort. Watch for lip movements the whole time.

Repeat this exercise six times.

EMPHASIS

Most people tire of listening very quickly. When talking to a buyer, this can result in the loss of a sale. We must, therefore, make sure that the sound of our words is more compelling. This means taking one word in a group of words and emphasising it. By doing this, we may change the meaning. For example, we can say, 'Thank you very much,' as a flat, disinterested piece of pseudo-courtesy, or we can say, 'Thank you *very* much.' This is much more personal.

The same applies to single words. 'No' can have many different meanings. Say 'No' to yourself now. It could mean a refusal, but put life in your voice and the *no* expresses surprise. Change the sound again and you can convey sympathy.

Coupled with emphasis is inflection, or the *tone* in the voice. A buyer will listen more intently if he hears a variety of sounds. For example, 'Will you be in your office in the morning?' can sound flat and uninteresting, but if you begin the 'Will you' on a high note, dropping to a lower tone at 'in the morning', you will have given light and shade to the whole sentence.

You can also emphasise syllables in words, almost putting them to music. You can say, 'It is exquisite,' meaning you are pleased with a design, but emphasise the *ex* or the *qui* and then you mean that the design is gorgeous.

BETTER COMMUNICATION

The professional telephone salesperson will study this chapter and immediately set about checking his voice and, if necessary, improving it. The amateur will not bother, believing that everyone understands every word he says. However monotonous his voice may be, he will believe it to be strong and resonant, forgetting that for the telephone salesperson his voice is his main selling tool.

No professional would play golf with a broken club. No snooker champion would use a bent cue. No telephone salesperson should sell with a voice that might impair the satisfactory conclusion of a sale.

There is a need for precision and quality in telephone selling if misunderstandings are to be avoided.

Your voice will register your mood, and your mood when telephone selling, must always be cheerful. Your enthusiasm must radiate over the wires. You are concerned with presenting your personality in words.

Colourful delivery is the expression of personality, and an expression of a vibrant personality is always good salespersonship.

CHAPTER 5

How to Get Appointments by Telephone

The salesperson's profitable time is the time she spends face to face with her customers and, of course, prospects, because few sales staff have all the customers they can handle. Most salespeople, therefore, while obtaining the maximum amount of business from their customers, must also seek out prospects to turn them into future customers.

In the industrial market, and even in the consumer field when contacting chain stores, she faces a problem: how to see those prospects who do not want to see her. Usually, her customers will see her. If they won't, then she has failed in her relationship with them, or something is wrong with her company's products. But obtaining an interview with a prospect needs a different technique from knocking on the door of one of her regular buyers.

What are her alternatives? She can cold call, or make an appointment by telephone.

Even if she is given enquiries to follow up, she will, more often than not, have to telephone for an appointment.

Cold calling will always have its place in selling and, in some forms of marketing, it is essential. However, it is usually a fill-in for the industrial salesperson. Rather than waste time between appointments, she will call cold on any nearby prospects. But cold calling as a planned system of working can be very time-consuming. For example, there can be long waits in reception areas until the prospect is disengaged. Also, a full day's work may result in only two good interviews, but telephoning in advance may enable a salesperson to make four or five appointments a day.

Preparation

The basis of all telephone selling – and making appointments by telephone is hard selling – must be good preparation. There are several rules to follow before making an appointment by telephone, and one golden rule is: *you must find out the prospect's name.*

Knowing the prospect's name will help you to handle her PA or receptionist and, by addressing your prospect by name, you are able to bring immediate warmth to the relationship with her.

It is important to use a name when selling face-to-face, but it is even more vital when trying to win a prospect over during a few minutes' telephone conversation. If all else fails and you cannot discover the prospect's name, then you must telephone her receptionist, ask for the name of the site manager (or whoever it is you want to speak to), thank him, and ring off because at this stage, if you ask to be put through, you may be questioned. You should then telephone again the next day.

The other rules are:

(a) You must have customer records available. These are important because they may contain information allowing you to anticipate a customer or prospect's reaction.

(b) A customer may have had a delivery complaint. A prospect might not have purchased previously because he – considered the price too high. With this knowledge available, you can forestall an objection to the interview.

(c) Directories, brochures, information screens, websites and any other information which you may need should be at hand. Names and telephone numbers for calls you intend to make should be on a list in front of you alongside, of course, pen and paper to make notes.

(d) Your diary is invaluable to you. Whenever possible, you will suggest days and times for the appointments to suit your convenience. Good appointment planning will leave time for cold calling on nearby prospects, or may even completely fill the day with appointments. You can only achieve these results by constant reference to your diary.

(e) Make sure that you will not be disturbed while telephoning. The emphasis is on *you*. You must never ask a PA or receptionist to get the prospect on the line for you.

Now, are you ready?

Making the Call

Pick up the telephone, dial the number and, on being greeted by the receptionist, ask to speak to Mr. Smith.

One of three things can happen:

a) The receptionist will transfer you immediately to Mr. Smith and all will be well.

b) The receptionist may ask you your business.

c) The receptionist may put you through to Mr. Smith's secretary.

To avoid (b) and (c), you must have an authoritative approach, e.g.:

> 'Will you please tell Mr. Smith, your financial director, that Angela White is on the line for him. Thank you.'

The *Angela* personalises the approach. Never use the prefix Ms or Mr. The *thank you* gives it a finality which does not invite a response. Unless the receptionist has special screening instructions regarding incoming calls, you will be put through to Mr. Smith.

Now we come to (b). The receptionist asks you for further information. You answer, quite simply:

'It is a business matter.'

Don't add anything further. It is not a misleading statement because it is a business matter which you can discuss only with Mr. Smith, the financial director.

Alternatively, it will show equal authority if you imply that you wish to discuss something of great importance. For example:

'It is in connection with Mr. Smith's financial planning.'

There is an excellent third approach if a letter has been sent in advance to the prospect, as either a personal letter or a direct mailer. You would then say:

'It is with reference to the letter I wrote to him.'

If the receptionist has been instructed to insist on obtaining information from every caller asking for Mr. Smith, you must then say:

'I am sorry, but it is a very involved matter. I think it would be best if you put me through to Mr. Smith's PA.'

It is sometimes advisable when making appointments to ask for a PA in the first place, but usually it is better to ask for the executive concerned. The PA may be away or out of her office and, in this event, the receptionist *may* put you straight through to the man you want to contact. If you do speak to the PA, however, either by your own request or because the receptionist has instructions, you will then have the selling task of persuading the PA to make an appointment for you to see Mr. Smith. You will use the selling principles outlined in the Telephone Sales Presentation, plus the golden words:

'I would like to ask your advice.'

You will not win every time, but you will win far more often than you will lose. In the majority of cases you will be able to speak to Mr. Smith.

Now, what do you say to him?

The Hook

There should, whenever possible, be a hook on which to hang your approach. This can be a letter which you or your company may have written, an advertisement, something new, a commercial on TV, a window display, or a reference from a friend or business associate. Your approach could be:

'Mr. Smith, this is Angela White of the Bridgewater Machine Tool Company. Have you a moment to speak on the telephone?'

This courtesy request, 'Have you a moment . . .' is not laid down as a fixed rule. It can, however, be very effective. It relaxes the prospect, because you have only asked him for a moment of his time. Also, it shows a courtesy that is lacking in so many telephone calls.

Whether you use this sentence or not, you must now repeat the prospect's name, after you have given him the name of your company.

Letter hook

'Mr. Smith, did you receive my letter?'
'No, what was it about?'

'Mr. Smith, it was about your car . . .'

(another example)
'Mr. Smith, did you receive my letter?'
'About your car washing system, wasn't it?'
'That's right. I want to call to see you, to explain . . .'

Advertisement hook
'Mr. Smith, did you see our advertisement in *The Engineering News*, announcing our new checking device which could help you so much to reduce costs . . .'

Reference hook
'Mr. Smith, we haven't met, but John Williams asked me to contact you . . .'

The Quick Approach Close
In all forms of selling, it is axiomatic that a salesperson should think of the close the minute the sale begins, but in telephone selling there is a difference. You can actually close at the approach. The prospect might be influenced by the name of your company, or interested in the product or service you are selling, or she likes the sound of your voice – you sound like someone she should listen to – or it may even be that she is very busy and arrives at a quick decision. Whatever the reason, this form of approach does get appointments. This is how to do it:

With conviction in your voice to create the impression that there cannot be a refusal, you say:
'Good morning Ms. Jones, this is Jack Smith of Halliday publications. I should like to take up just eight minutes of your time to tell you about our new journal for your industry and its wonderful advertis-

ing pull. Would Wednesday morning or Wednesday afternoon be more convenient for me to call?'

This approach covers a lot if ground. It is brief. It asks for only a short interview. It states your business, and it closes.

The Question Hook

When you haven't a hook of any kind, then ask a question:

Mr. Smith, this is Mike Boon of the Bessing Group. Have you heard of our organisation?'

Whether you receive the reply 'yes' or 'no' is immaterial, because it will take you smoothly into the main reason for your call.

Be Special

A wonderful word to use in all approaches is *special*, or *specially* –

'Mr. Smith, I am calling you specially to tell you about . . .'

'Ms. Jones, there is a special reason why I should like to see you . . .'

Keep to the Rules

Although the quick close will get you interviews, in many cases there will be a request for further information. Here are some points to remember:

- Time is not on your side, so keep the benefits short.
- You must not become involved in a full presentation.
- Keep the objective in mind: *to obtain an interview.*
- You must use short sentences.
- You must use understandable words.
- You must be authoritative, but never talk down to

the prospect.

- You must not try to be too clever. You have to persuade the prospect that you are a sincere person by the words you use, and by the tone of your voice.
- You must have a reason for not giving full information over the telephone, e.g., samples to be shown, a model of a building to examine, figures to analyse, a drawing to discuss, or matters so personal that they should be discussed face-to-face.

You may also have to evaluate the prospect, if his buying potential is not known. It is time-wasting to make an appointment with a prospect who seems interested in office partitioning if his offices are small, brick-built, and he is not allowed by his landlord to knock down the walls. If you are selling a property trust bond plus insurance, and to make the policy worthwhile the prospect has to invest a minimum of £1,000, then you will have to discover whether he has this cash available.

Evaluation is best carried out when the prospect has shown interest in your proposal, and you know you will get an appointment. You can then use the question technique.

The salesperson selling partitioning could say:

'Can you tell me the approximate size of your main office?'

The insurance salesperson may be quite direct:

'Mr. Smith, if you were shown how you could add 50% to your capital, are you prepared to put down £1,000?'

You can always back out of an interview by saying,

'Mr. Smith, perhaps I had better send you literature first.'

The telephone salesperson will only withdraw from the interview if she is certain the customer either cannot afford her product or service, or, within the foreseeable future, will not be in the market for it.

The Main Benefit

You must stake your claim for an interview in a few compelling words:

- 'I'd like to show you some recent information on . . .'
- 'You will want to consider six ideas for cutting down overheads in your offices . . .'
- 'We have designed a very unusual saving plan which will be of great benefit to you . . .'
- 'The personal organiser is no bigger than your calculator. Knowing something of your company's activities, you would find this of tremendous help for personal use . . .'
- 'You would want to handle the equipment yourself, to see how well it works . . .'

Your aim is to intrigue the prospect, to interest her so that she will want to hear more and will give you an interview.

The Objections

What could her objections be? She can hardly object to your product or service, because you have only given her the barest outline. She can only object to you taking up her time at an interview.

What can happen? She can answer:

- 'I'll see you,' and all will be well.
- 'Send me the information.'

- 'Tell me now.
- 'I'm too busy.'

There are several ways of tackling the request for further information.

- 'Mr. Smith, you may want to see proof of how a company has been able to increase overall production by up to 28%.'
- 'Mr. Brown, I want to talk to you about a new way in which you can protect your money and beat inflation. Would next Tuesday morning . . .'
- 'Ms. Jones, you demand a very fast delivery service. We can provide that at low cost, and you will want to examine this claim. It is for this reason that I want the opportunity of meeting you. May I call . . .'
- 'I cannot advise you, Ms. Black, until I know one or two things about your company . . .'
- 'You would need to look at our analysis forms, Mr. Clark. I'll bring them with me. It will only take a few minutes. May I call on . . .'

To the statement, 'I am too busy', the salesperson has several answers, according to what he is selling, e.g.:

- 'That is why I am telephoning you, Mr. Smith, because I know you are so busy. I can help you in this direction by cutting down some of the demands on your time.'

Ego-building can also be a sound policy.

- 'Mr. White, I have found that it is busy people like you who are most interested . . .'

Or assume that the prospect is only encountering a temporary rush of business.

- 'Of course, Ms. Howell, I know how busy you are. I was not thinking of disturbing you today or tomorrow. Will you be able to see me on Thursday or Friday of next week?'

If she still persists that she is busy, then an unusual request could be made:

- 'It is because you are so busy that I feel my proposition will have real value for you. Perhaps I can help you personally. May I call to see you outside business hours? Either early in the morning, or later in the evening – say six or seven p.m. – which would you prefer?'

Surprisingly, this unusual request is very often quite acceptable. If you do see the prospect after office hours, you will find him more relaxed and receptive to your ideas than when he is involved in the rush and bustle of a busy office.

If you reach a point where you feel you are antagonising the prospect, then you must never shut the door to a future appointment. Say, 'I'll call you again in a fortnight's time, Mr. Smith.'

If this does not work, there is always one final request which you can make. It is rarely refused:

- 'Mr. Smith, there are some times of the day when you are not so busy as others, although I appreciate that you cannot specify them. When I am near your offices, may I call on the off-chance of seeing you?'

He will nearly always say 'yes', and this is noted in your cold calling diary.

Following the telephone call, after two or three visits at the most, you will find that you will see Mr. Smith.

The Close

Tying up an appointment is different from locking up an order, when you can use any of the closes set out in the sales presentation. This is not possible when selling the interview. Nearly always, therefore, you will use the *alternative close*, based on an appointment time.

Most salespeople suggest a time for a meeting on the hour or the half-hour. You can be different. Put forward 9.10 a.m. or 3.50 p.m. The very unexpected nature of this suggestion will often bring its own reward. But the main reason for using this technique is that many busy people make appointments on the hour or half-hour, some of which will last for the full period, and others will be cut short. The odd time, therefore, will often appeal to the prospect whose appointments on the hour may leave him periods in between which are free.

And remember, you are only asking for a few minutes of his time, knowing that if you interest him, he will ask you to remain.

Another factor adds value to the odd-time appointment: it indicates to the prospect that you are a busy person, and that you are fitting him into your full day's schedule of appointments.

The Close, therefore, can be:

'Will Wednesday or Thursday suit you best, Mr. Lovell?'
'Er – Wednesday.'
'Morning or afternoon?'

'Afternoon is best for me.'

'That's fine, Mr. Lovell. Then can you make it two-ten, or would four-fifty be more convenient?'

'Ten past two would suit me.'

'Thank you, Mr. Lovell, I'll look forward to meeting you at ten past two on Wednesday.'

Keep on Closing

Do you remember the story of the old-time salesperson who kept seven coins in his pocket? At every refusal to buy, he would transfer one coin to another pocket. If he had not got the order by the time the seventh coin had been moved, he would pack up and go.

He claimed that he rarely had to take more than four or five coins away, even when selling to the most difficult customers. He believed in the salesperson's creed: *Never give up; keep trying.*

In telephone selling, there isn't the time to ask for the order seven times, but you can ask two or three times. This is how it is done:

Example A

The following technique shows how an insurance salesperson can keep asking for an appointment:

'Good morning, Ms. Swift, my name is Jack Barclay of World Insurance Company. I would like to take up just nine minutes of your time to tell you about our Executive Plan. Would next Tuesday morning, or Thursday afternoon at 2.50 p.m., be more convenient?'

'What's it all about?'

'Mr. Swift, it's to show you how you can increase your capital – a fascinating subject, I'm sure you will agree. Would Tuesday or Thursday . . .' (first trial close).

'You want to sell me insurance?'
'Are you interested in insurance?'
'No.'
'What I want to talk about, Mr. Swift, is a new way you can protect your money and beat inflation. Would Tuesday morning . . .' (second trial close).

'I haven't any money to invest.'
'Mr. Swift, all I am asking you to invest is nine minutes of your time. Would Tuesday morning . . .' (third trial close).

More often than not, the appointment will be given after the first, second, or third close. One golden rule to observe is: *keep command of the conversation*. If the prospect takes charge, you will lose the interview.

Here is another variation of this presentation:

'Good morning, Mr. Swift, my name is Jack Barclay of World Insurance Company. I should like to take up just nine minutes of your time to tell you about our Executive Plan. Would next Tuesday morning or Thursday afternoon at 2.50 p.m., be more convenient?'
'I'm not interested.'
'Mr. Swift, I realise that you will not be interested until I have told you about the Executive Plan. Would Tuesday or Thursday be more convenient?'
'I haven't time to discuss personal matters at my office. I'm far too busy.'
'Mr. Swift, may I ask you a question? Like most people today, you save money in one way or another, don't you?'
'Well, yes.'

'Good. Now if there were a scheme available that gave you a higher return for your money than your present saving plan, you would want to know about it, wouldn't you?'

'Of course.'

'Fine! That is just what I want to talk to you about. Now would Tuesday morning . . .'

This technique of asking a question and diverting attention from the objection is a good technique for obtaining an appointment.

Example B
(The salesperson of Arrow Industrial Weighing Machine Company is telephoning a Production Director, seeking an appointment.)

'Mrs. Harvey? Good morning, this is Peter Lisle of The Arrow Weighing Machine Company. We met some three years ago when the maintenance contract on your weighing equipment was arranged. Can you spare me a moment?'

'Yes.'

'Mrs. Harvey, the contract is due for renewal next month. You will want to see the new proposal, so may I call on Wednesday . . .?'

'There's no need for you to come here. You can post the papers on to me.'

'Thank you, Mrs. Harvey, but reports from my engineers show that certain machines are being used either less or more than they were three years ago. You will agree that we should try to relate the frequency of maintenance on each machine to its use and importance. On Wednesday, I can explain . . .'

'You'd be better talking to my chief engineer about this. He'll know what he wants, and I will accept his recommendations, provided the charge for the contract isn't any higher than before. Costs seem to keep rising.'

'They do indeed, Mrs. Harvey, and you'll understand that in providing a service, a very high proportion of the premium is directly related to labour costs – and we both know how wages keep going up. In any event, you and I can work this out between us, and I'm sure you'll agree that we should have a talk about it. Would Wednesday . . .?'

Particular Points

1. Reason for call made clear. Mrs. Harvey *might* have agreed to see the salesperson without more discussion.
2. A valid, although secondary, reason for wanting an appointment.
3. The primary reason comes out but is not dealt with, as Peter Lisle does not want to become involved in a price discussion. The need for the meeting is brought to a 'you and I' situation. Lisle has raised the importance of the issue, and has built up the ego of Mrs. Harvey.

Conclusion

To succeed in obtaining more appointments by telephone, you must:

- Know your prospects and their business.
- Have a definite reason for asking for the interview.
- Have a planned approach.
- Have a main benefit to stress the need for the appointment.

- Be prepared to listen, and don't pounce (It might be that the prospect is about to give you an interview when you interrupt.).
- Smile when you talk on the telephone.
- Talk a little more slowly than usual.
- If not making headway, ask questions.
- Sound enthusiastic – your enthusiasm will vibrate over the wires and will do more than anything else to get that appointment for you.

The obtaining of appointments is a challenge to all salespeople – a challenge which, if accepted, can lead to a far greater volume of business.

CHAPTER 6
Dial Human Relations

We can dial a telephone number and receive advice, news, weather reports, sporting results, recipes and the latest stock market prices. If, however, BT were to advertise *dial 1111 for improved human relations*, it would be taken out of service within a few months because of non-usage.

Why would it fail?

1. Because we all believe that we get along splendidly with everyone, and therefore we need no guidance on this subject.
2. We do not agree with the fundamentals of human relations, thinking that it may mean being hypocritical.
3. In this tough modern world, we imagine there is no time for the niceties.
4. We believe people must take us as they find us.

Let me make one thing clear: if all the books in the world on Human Relations were placed end-to-end, they *might* stretch far enough to reach the one man or woman who follows all of their advice.

As we are human beings with human frailties, all we can do is to strive for a better understanding of ourselves and other people. From this understanding stems the ability to *get along with people*.

There would be no necessity to press home the need for human relations in telephone selling if it were not for the stances taken by so many people under the above four categories.

Does the ill-mannered hotel receptionist ever believe that she is in the wrong? Of course not. It is those woeful, polite, subservient strangers in the queue, waiting to see if they can obtain accommodation, who are always discourteous and demanding. Does the snapping, tight-lipped shop assistant believe that she is rude? Of course not. She is a paragon of virtue in her own eyes, and, if only other shop assistants she meets when she goes shopping were like her, all would be well in the retail world.

Every telephone salesperson must be introspective enough and honest enough to be able to pinpoint his human relations weaknesses.

Good human relations does not mean being weak or subservient. It only means acting towards others as we should like them to act towards us.

The salesperson who says, 'They must take me as they find me' might discover that no one wants to take her anywhere.

No buyer would say to a telephone salesperson:

'You sound belligerent.'

'You are argumentative.'

'You are impolite.'

'You are too familiar.'

They have a far better way of showing their criticism: they put down the receiver, and don't buy.

It is true that in this modern, tough business world there is no room for niceties if, by niceties, we mean unctuous flattery, but there is always time for courtesy. Interestingly, usually it is rude, blunt, curt people who expect the most courtesy from others.

Why should anyone buy from us – or agree to our requests for immediate payment of an account or accept our excuses for non-delivery of goods – if they feel antagonistic towards us?

Someone once said that the only man who can afford to forget human relations in marketing is the one with a monopoly, with traders beating down his door for supplies. But monopolies are few and far between these days, and they rarely last. Most salespeople have strong competition.

The way to beat the opposition is to have the best possible sales presentation, plus a likeable personality. Over the telephone, a prospect only warms to us because she likes either our voice, our attitude or the choice of words we use.

Good Telephone Manners

What do *good manners* conjure up in your mind? A heavily built, well-fed Victorian gentleman saying to his wife, 'The gel will have to go – she doesn't know her place'? Or Lady Highmost writing to *The Times* to complain that young people these days don't stand to attention when she enters a room?

In fact, having good manners does not mean being servile, and to be ill-mannered is not the prerogative of the young. Many people are not intentionally discourteous, but they do lack awareness.

The telephone salesperson must have that awareness, because good telephone manners win customers.

Don't you quickly reach boiling point when someone treats you brusquely, stares through you, keeps mispronouncing your name, belittles you, or behaves curtly? Of course you do!

You may now ask, 'What is this all about? This book is about telephone selling, not moral values.'

One goes with the other. If we are not conscious that we irritate and annoy people, how can we influence them to our way of thinking?

Let us take a few examples of bad manners, or lack of courtesy in telephone selling:

We can smoke or eat a biscuit while telephoning, and if you think this is unusual, you haven't seen many telephone sales staff at work, or listened to someone munching at the other end of the line.

When a salesperson speaks with a cigarette dangling from his mouth, he can strain the hearing of the prospect, trying to catch the muddled sounds hissing past half-closed lips. 'Sorry', says the salesperson, who inhales deeply, splutters, and coughs. That would be all right if he were selling coughs.

It is bad manners to be overfamiliar with a receptionist, thinking that that will win her over.

It is bad manners to mispronounce somebody's name.

It is discourteous to ask a prospect to hold on while the telephone salesperson searches for a price list.

In spite of what the cynics say, people do appreciate good manners. And remember, *we* are *they* to our prospects and customers.

Politeness never yet lost the telephone salesperson an order. Lack of it, however, has caused many a telephone to be slammed down.

It Travels

An old song contains the words, *a smile will go a long, long way.* The song writer wasn't thinking of a telephone call when he wrote those words, but, amazing as it may seem, a smile does travel. If the caller smiles, the listener can 'hear' it in the voice.

The telephone salesperson must not only smile, but she must act as if she is selling face-to-face. If you grimace, gesticulate or raise your eyebrows, the listener can pick up on it just from the tone of the caller's voice. This is because we alter the tone of our voice when we smile, or become annoyed.

Most people do smile often when they speak on the telephone. A mother, talking to her daughter, will automatically smile when told of what that little scamp of a grandson did this morning, and the daughter knows her mother is smiling.

You *can* communicate a smile. Byron wrote:

And o'er that cheek, and o'er that brou'
So soft, so calm, yet eloquent
The smiles that win . . .

Byron was not thinking of the telephone salesperson, but for all that, smiles do help to win orders.

Enthusiasm

We all know that there is nothing so contagious as enthusiasm – except the lack of it. If the telephone salesperson cannot be enthusiastic about his product or service, he should find another job. This applies particularly when he is trying to make an appointment. If you make your proposition sound a great opportunity for the prospect, she will see you. If she feels that you are just making another routine call, she will not interrupt her routine to make an appointment with you.

The enthusiastic salesperson not only smiles when selling, but his eyes light up because he is enjoying himself.

When Edison was developing the incandescent light,

he kept on experimenting and would not be sidetracked. After some thirty thousand experiments, he had still not succeeded. One of his assistants lost his enthusiasm and said, 'Mr. Edison, why go on? We have made thirty thousand experiments and we are no nearer the results.'

'No nearer the results!' shouted Edison with great enthusiasm, 'We've had marvellous results! We now know thirty thousand things which won't work.'

The telephone salesperson must always remember that he needs his enthusiasm most when the going is tough. Enthusiasm, more than anything else, can turn an average salesperson into a super-salesperson, because it is that enthusiasm which will urge him to improve his presentation, improve his speaking voice and master the techniques of telephone selling.

Tact

There is a Chinese proverb on tactlessness: *although there exist many thousand subjects for conversation, there are persons who cannot meet a cripple without talking about his feet.*

Tactlessness in any walk of life is harmful. In telephone selling, it is an order loser.

It is tactless to be too familiar.

It is tactless to use first names even when the buyer makes the first gesture, without his invitation to use his first name.

It is tactless – and racist – to make remarks when selling such as:

'That sounds a bit Irish.'

'You must be a Scotsman – you drive a hard bargain.'

Jewish people are not won over when the telephone salesperson uses Jewish expressions, and the Welshman doesn't want to be reminded that *Taffy was a Welshman*.

It is tactless to correct a word wrongly pronounced by the prospect, by giving the correct pronunciation immediately afterwards.

It is tactless to . . .

There are a million of 'em, as 1950's American comedian Jimmy Durante used to say. Don't you use any one of them.

Listen

Of all the self-disciplines we need for succeeding in selling, the discipline of listening more and talking less is one of the hardest to master.

The reason is obvious. We are always so interesting; we have such a fine story to tell; we always intrigue our listeners; we are so humorous; we had such a wonderful holiday; we had such a strange experience; AND, the other fellow is such a bore. It is so hard for us to understand that the other person feels just like we do.

When friends are battling for talk time, the one who is least sensitive always wins. You have to be insensitive to other people's feelings to be able to pump word after word at them and not give them a break for a reply.

The salesperson with the funny-man complex wants you to hear his stories, yet he always wants to cap yours before you reach the punchline. The articulate crusader – regardless of what she is crusading for – will not give you time for her ideas to be answered. That's life.

Now we don't change our spots when we become telephone salespeople: the funny-man or the insensitive crusader will still want to monopolise the conversation.

It doesn't matter much in everyday conversation. The worst thing that can happen is that our friends avoid us.

However, in telephone selling, if you are unable to be a good listener you can quickly become a good loser.

There is an old tag that goes: *You don't have bad prospects, they have a bad listener.*

Never finish a prospect's sentence for him. Don't let your impatience show with 'yes, yes' interruptions; they are commands for him to speak more quickly. Never attempt to over-talk the prospect. Let him be solo; don't make it a duet.

Intent listening will help you to pick up the buying signals. Also, if he talks, he is interested. When he stops talking, he has put down the telephone.

When the conversation is two-way, you know that he is involved in the sales presentation. You can 'listen' yourself into appointments and sales. Listen most of all when you have asked a question. If you have talked through the answer, you may have misunderstood what the prospect has said. You may continue selling when the sale is ready for closing.

I once asked a psychiatrist why people talk too much. I could not understand his reply, because he talked for twenty minutes without a break using psychological jargon which he understood, but I did not. When he had finished, I said, 'That was all foreign to me. Can you sum it up in a couple of words?'

'That,' he answered, 'would be like asking a government department to simplify a law. There can be no simplification, but if you want a generalisation, then the person who talks too much does so from fear – fear of stopping and not being able to restart, fear of appearing inferior, fear of the interruption that he cannot handle.'

If it is true that we can only conquer fear by recognising it, then perhaps recognition might help the non-listener to talk less and to listen more.

You will recollect that in the chapter on *Voice Projection* it was explained that by emphasising a word, by altering the sound of words, you can change meanings. This applies just as much to the prospect as to the salesperson.

The prospect might say, 'Really, I don't want it,' which might sound half-hearted. It could also be a buying signal.

But if the prospect snapped *really*, and then emphasized *don't*, you might as well ring off.

By half-listening, the first sound from the prospect could be mistaken for the second, and the salesperson might then ring off when the order was just around the corner.

Listening can be called an art, but it is an art which can be acquired by all telephone salespeople. It only needs consideration – consideration first of what you are saying, and then equal consideration of what the prospect is saying, or asking. A good listener wins respect, achieves a friendly relationship with her customers, and learns the lesson that the easiest way to sell is to allow the prospect to buy.

Little Things Mean a Lot

It always delights us when meeting someone again after a period of time has elapsed and he says, 'I remember you very well; you had just started work for Smith & Sons and you were very happy. Also, I remember the day we met was your first wedding anniversary.'

We almost shout with pleasure as we answer, 'What a fantastic memory!'

Most of us haven't got a good memory, so in business we have to rely on diaries, secretaries, notepads, etc. The telephone salesperson should always keep her records up to date. This applies not only to the orders she receives, but to repeat orders, special sales promotions, and any information relative to the buyer, the buyer's secretary, and other members of her staff. If, by chance, the buyer should say, 'I'm celebrating this evening – it's my birthday, but don't ask me how old I am,' make a note of it. A year later on that day, you can wish her a happy birthday.

If her PA is going on holiday, make a note. When she returns and you are speaking to her on the telephone, ask her how she enjoyed her trip abroad.

If the buyer has been away ill, show interest in her illness when she returns. But remember, it must be a sincere interest – and not relayed as if with an on-and-off switch. It does no good to ask after her health and then, before she has finished detailing her sufferings, to interrupt with a business-related remark.'

It is not time-wasting to make personal enquiries of the buyer and her staff. It is only time-wasting when you talk about *your* holiday, or *your* illness. She is not interested in you, but you are interested in her for two reasons: the first, because it is good business; the second, because a habit, good or bad, can develop into being an integral part of a complicated human being. What sometimes begins as an act of salesmanship can become a part of our nature, and we are all better for being really interested in other people.

Human Relations

As mentioned earlier, thousands of books have been written on the subject of human relations. They have been written by social workers, teachers of religion, psychiatrists, psychologists, behavioural scientists, and lovers of humanity. Although they don't agree on all aspects of human relations, they mostly concur on one truism: *we like people to like us*. But the salesperson doesn't have to sell her soul to be liked. All she has to do is to stop antagonising others, so that she won't be disliked.

Everyone can master the basic principles of human relations in telephone selling. They are so simple:

Be courteous.

Smile when you talk.

Be enthusiastic.

Be tactful.

Be a good listener.

Be reliable.

Remember little things.

CHAPTER 7

Answering Objections

There is still a school of thought which advocates the old theory of welcoming objections as proof that the prospect is interested and is seeking further information. The prospect, according to this thinking, may even want to buy, and is using the objection as a challenge, to eliminate the possibility of making a mistake.

Modern opinion disagrees with this viewpoint. Unless a very weak objection is raised, the prospect is making a point which the salesperson must destroy. For example, the objection might be:

'I can buy cheaper elsewhere.'

The standard answer to this objection is to prove to the prospect that he doesn't only buy on price. There must be other factors such as quality, delivery, service and confidence in the supplier. The price differential is narrowed and it is proved to the prospect that he should not consider the price of the product, which may be £50, against one that he can buy for £45. All he has to consider is the £5 difference, and the benefits he is getting for that £5. A good, sensible argument and one which will succeed time and time again, but the salesperson is still implying that the prospect is naive, doesn't understand his job, lacks business sense, and is indecisive, which sometimes can make a prospect dig his heels in and refuse to buy even when he knows that his objection is not valid. Therefore, never welcome objections – always try to forestall them. Provided the prospect only *thinks* the objection, no harm is done if he is proved wrong. It is when he *voices* it that he is likely to stand his ground. The telephone salesperson should, therefore, build into his presentation answers to possible objections. This is the strength of the selling sentence technique. The elaboration of the step which will follow the sentence can so easily be changed.

If, for example, you know that your product has a feature which the prospect might consider to be a weakness, incorporate this weakness as a selling point. When you know that the prospect will raise an objection because of bad service received from your company in the past, bring it out into the open yourself. For example:

> 'Mr. Lee, as you know we have, in the past, had difficulties in meeting your delivery schedules. It is a problem which faces every company now and again, and it caused me a considerable amount of worry on your behalf. You will be delighted to know, Mr. Lee, that I can now assure you that you will receive supplies within three days of ordering.'

The salesperson, having raised and overcome the objection, will continue immediately with his sales presentation. He must never pause to allow Mr. Lee to make any comment about bad deliveries. Best of all, he should switch to a question which in no way refers to the delivery problem, for instance: 'By the way, Mr. Lee, do you still find red is in demand?'

The salesperson will now have achieved a dual object. He has forestalled the objection, and has taken the prospect's mind away from it by asking a question on another subject.

Here is another example:

> 'Ms. Jenkins, you have the reputation of being a very

keen buyer, may I ask you a question?'
'Yes.'
'Do you buy *only* on price?'

No buyer will give an unqualified 'yes' to this. The answer will most probably be:
'No, I buy on value.'

The salesperson can then continue:
'That's fine, Ms. Jenkins, because it is value I want
to talk about.'

Some salespeople invite objections by breaking fundamental rules of telephone salesmanship. Here are the pitfalls to avoid:

Do not ask irrelevant questions
All too often a salesperson will ask a question which invites a negative response. For example:
'Is the line selling well?'

Whether it is or not, the buyer, fearful of adding to his stocks, sees an easy way out and replies:
'No, I'm afraid it's sticking. Ring me again next week.'

Do not ask questions which can annoy the prospect
It is so easy to upset someone who is not keen to buy or to make an appointment. For example:
'Mr. Brown, you cater for the lower end of the trade, don't you?'

The salesperson may well have slotted Mr. Brown's business in the right category, but Mr. Brown may like to mislead himself into believing that he also has a good class trade. He will, therefore, disagree with the salesperson, and cut the conversation short.

Here is another example:
'Ms. Jones, you would like your office to be more productive, wouldn't you?'

Ms. Jones would, but she will rarely admit directly that there is room for improvement in her offices.

Be certain you can handle replies to questions

During research for this book, I heard a telephone salesperson saying:

'I'll call any time to suit, Mr. X. When may I come along?'

'Thursday, 8 a.m.'

Pause.

'I'm sorry, I'm afraid I can't manage that.'

Another example is:

'You can have any colour you like, Mr. X.'

'I'll have black.'

'Oh, that's one we don't do now. There's no demand . . .'

Answering Objections

In spite of your care in preparing your presentation, including asking the right questions, you will still get objections. Your planning is to minimise them. There are techniques for handling difficult objections.

They can only come under one of five headings:

1. Not interested
2. Can't afford it
3. Can buy better elsewhere
4. Dissatisfied with previous transaction
5. Delay-excuses.

All objections are derived from these five main reasons for not buying.

1. '*Not interested*' can mean:
    – 'Not interested in your product'
    – 'Not interested in any similar product'
    – 'Not interested because your price is too high'

- 'Not interested because you have a technically inferior product . . .'

2. If the need is present and the objection is, '*cannot afford it*,' it can mean that the prospect cannot afford to buy it from you, because:
   - He is temporarily short of cash.
   - It is out of his price range.
   - He would buy if it were cheaper.
   - He could buy later.

3. '*Can buy better elsewhere*' could mean:
   - Your quality is not good enough
   - Others have better designs
   - It does not meet with his specification.

4. *Dissatisfaction with previous transactions* might be a result of:
   - Difficulty in obtaining deliveries
   - Being unduly pressed for payment
   - Having had service problems . . .

5. *Delay-excuses:*
   - The prospect wants to consult his partner, director, a member of his family, experts, professional advisers, etc., etc.

The telephone salesperson must evolve skills to answer these objections.

Hear It Out

Let the prospect voice her objection in full. In spite of the limitation of time you must not *pounce*, because of your eagerness to tell her that she is wrong. Let her expound on her objection; she may even sell herself off it. For example:

'I made up my mind not to deal with your people again. Your representative definitely misled me, and I couldn't even get an apology from your sales manager. I'm not blaming you – you've only just joined the company.'

The prospect is giving the salesperson an immediate opportunity to ease the customer back into a selling situation, firstly by ego-building:

'Ms. James, it is very good of you to say that. You are obviously a fair person, and I am sure, therefore, that you will see me for a few minutes to allow me to explain how things have changed, and how we can now be of better service to you. May I call . . .?'

Keep Quiet

There is something very dramatic about a pause, and something very disconcerting about silence over the telephone. If you wait for a few seconds before replying, there is always the possibility that the prospect will add to her objection and give you the hidden objection – the true reason for her not buying.

Repeat the Objection

Be sure that you understand the objection. The prospect is not taught to obtain 'yes' responses. She can only assume that you and she are both on the same wave length.

'There is no point in my seeing you; I'm full up with insurance. I'm getting on in age, and I've only got myself to think about.'

But the salesperson doesn't listen carefully. She only hears the first few words, 'I'm full up with insurance' – a standard objection to which he immediately gives the standard reply:

'I'm sure you will agree, Ms. James, that you would increase your insurance if I could show you how your policies could be rearranged. You might even save money.'

But the main point raised by the prospect was, 'I have only myself to think about,' and that should have been the link on which the salesperson should have based his reply, as in the following:

> 'Ms. James, I appreciate that as a good businessman you are carrying a lot of insurance, and that you have only yourself to think about.' (Pause here for any correction, then continue:) 'I assume that you are a widow, Ms. James?'
>
> 'Yes.'
>
> 'Have you any children?'
>
> 'They're all grown up.
>
> 'Grandchildren?'
>
> 'Yes.'
>
> 'Well that's fine then, Ms. James, because that is one of the things I want to talk to you about – how you can safeguard your future – and one doesn't know one's span of life, or how inflation will take its toll on income. Also, there is a special benefit that you can confer on your grandchildren without affecting your own income. May I call . . .?'

By repeating the objection, he takes the sting out of it, but, more important, he makes certain that he has understood it, and that he can, therefore, answer it completely.

Acknowledge the buyer's viewpoint
Whenever an objection is raised, tension creeps in. No buyer will admit it, but we all have a sense of caution that makes us tense before we arrive at a decision. Therefore, the salesperson must relax the buyer. The buyer raises the

objection and expects an argument. The salesperson also tenses as he senses the order veering away from him. To take the tension out of the objection, the telephone salesperson should acknowledge the buyer's viewpoint.

In a few words, he indicates that he is inclined to agree with the prospect. The prospect, scenting victory, relaxes.

This technique is based on empathy with the buyer. Although the words may vary, the application is always the same, e.g.:

- 'I quite appreciate the reason for your thinking that it would take up too much space, but . . .'
- 'You are quite right, Mr. Thomas, in thinking that because the circulation is limited you would not get results, but . . .'
- 'Mr. Smith, it is quite true that extra labour might be required, but . . .'

By acknowledging the buyer's viewpoint, you can take the tension out of the objection.

Praise the Prospect
When you link courtesy to ego-building, the objection will not loom so large in the prospect's mind. Use these words:

- 'That is a very good point, Mr. Smith . . .'
- 'I appreciate the very fair way . . .'
- 'You are a very keen buyer, Ms. Jenkins, and I understand your objection to opening an account with a relatively small company, but . . .'
- 'I know that a person in your position is always very busy, but I only need ten minutes to explain . . .'

Ask Questions
You can turn an objection into a sales point by asking a question.

'I'll speak to my partner about it.'

'That is a good idea, Mr. Brown. Were there particular points you wanted to discuss with him?'

*   *   *

'I don't want any more insurance.'

'So you are completely happy with your level of insurance at the moment, Ms. Smith.'

*   *   *

'We're overstocked.'

'But you do like our products, Mr. Johnson?'

'Yes.'

'And you will stock them again when your stock levels are lower?'

'Of course.'

'Then your only concern is about placing an order now?'

'Yes.'

'That's fine. We can look ahead together and plan for future deliveries. May I call to see you . . .?'

*   *   *

'I can't afford a new freezer.'

'I appreciate that, but you are interested in saving money, Ms. Loveday, aren't you? And if I could show you that a freezer could pay for itself over a period of time, you would consider the proposition, wouldn't you? May I call . . .?'

The professional salesperson never welcomes objections, but, by a complete analysis of his product or service, he either forestalls the objection, or knows the technique to use as the occasion demands.

The following are extracts from calls made by telephone salespeople showing how they handle objections:

(a) *Overcoming Difficult Situations*

Some commercial markets are dominated by delivery, service and price considerations. Differences between suppliers are minimal. This situation applies to many products or services.

In these circumstances, a common objection to applications for initial interviews is *satisfaction with the existing supplier*. A successful approach is often achieved by recognising the prospect's objection (due to market knowledge, a survey, and observation) before he presents it, as in the scenario below:

'Mr. Harris, you demand and get a fast delivery service on your petrol and diesel requirements. It is for that very reason I would appreciate the opportunity of meeting you. This is Larry Williams of the Apex Oil Company.'

'You're right about delivery, but price also matters. I've got to get a good rebate.'

'Of course, Mr. Harris, and I know you get both these requirements from your existing suppliers.'

'I do. I've dealt with them for nearly ten years now, and I expect to go on buying from them for the next ten years.'

'Your loyalty is praiseworthy, Mr. Harris. Have you considered the situation should any one of a variety of reasons prevent your suppliers from delivering on time – reasons possibly beyond their control? Can you risk your business coming to a stop?'

'You've got a point there.'

'Look, Mr. Harris, let me come along to ensure that we have a record of your product requirements, delivery points and current rebates. Then we can agree trading terms so that you can count on your needs being met should any emergency arise.'

'Yes, that's a good idea.'

'May I call on . . .?'

(b) *Delay-Excuses*

'Good morning Ms. Young, this is Harold Lester of ABC Insurance Brokers. I should very much like the opportunity of meeting you. May I call –

'What do you want to see me about?'

'Ms. Young, I want to show you how our company has been able to reduce total insurance premiums by up to 30% for some twelve thousand eight hundred companies not only in the U.K. but throughout the U.S.A. and Europe.'

'It sounds interesting, but we are so busy at this time of the year with audits. Come and see me in about three months.'

Ms. Young, you are probably paying more than you need to right now. If I can guarantee immediate savings in premiums this would interest you, wouldn't it, Ms. Young? May I call . . .'

(c) *Not Interested*

'This, Mr. Prospect, I can well appreciate. But that is exactly what many of my clients said when first I spoke to them. You will appreciate that I cannot explain my proposition over the telephone, and it is for this reason that it would be in your interest for us to meet and see how you can benefit, as many others have already done. Now initially I don't require very much of your time. Would Thursday at 2.20 p.m. be suitable, or Friday morning at 10.20?'

(d)   *Send Details in the Post*

'Yes, Ms. Williams, I will certainly send a brochure to you describing the general background of my company, and how we have helped many other people like yourself. This will enable you to acquire background information on our service, and when we meet I shall be able to show you exactly how we can help you specifically. Would Wednesday or Thursday suit you?'

'I am sure, Mr. Brown, that you are already receiving a great many brochures through the post and they can be most useful in detailing a proposition generally. I know you will agree, however, that our service is so personal to you and your requirements that it would be far better if I could show you how we can help you. May I call?'

The prospect will listen more readily to your presentation if he can save face and still maintain his authority. He saves face when you forestall his objection, or when you use a technique which, instead of making him more stubborn, makes him ready to agree with you.

CHAPTER 8

Incoming Calls

A first impression means so much. Often, quite irrationally, we like or dislike a person on sight. Messages flash through the mind that:
- she's putting on airs
- he's acting a part
- she looks bitchy to me
- he's too dynamic for my liking, etc.

How ridiculous it is to come to such conclusions on such little evidence. Our judgement is so often proved wrong.

Have you ever taken an instant dislike to a fellow holiday-maker, only to find that you have been mistaken – he's actually quite nice? Generally, however, we are not given the opportunity to fathom the true man behind the façade. We go on our way, disliking him forever.

Our attitude towards companies can be coloured just as quickly. When we telephone a store and are greeted curtly, told to hold on and, neglected, we begin by being angry with the receptionist and end by damning the entire store.

Every incoming telephone call is a sales opportunity – an opportunity to win goodwill, smooth down the feathers of a dissatisfied customer, help build the morale of a salesperson, or obtain an order. In every case, a mind must be influenced, and that is what selling is about.

The receptionist is given the first opportunity of creating the right impression. That can be difficult for her if she is sitting, cramped, in a dingy, draughty reception. If receptionists are to give their best, they should work in bright surroundings, be comfortably seated, and be left alone. All too often, the reception area is a meeting place for other members of the staff who want to gossip.

On joining a company, the receptionist should be given a booklet of helpful advice. This could include the following information:

(a) Always realise that you are one of the most important members of our staff, and that you can do a great deal to help our business to run smoothly.

(b) Calls for executives should be put through directly to the executive concerned unless special instructions have been given for them to be accepted by a PA.

(c) The recipient of the call – departmental staff PA, or executive – will wish to greet the caller by name. If you do not know their name, ask for it in the following manner:

'May I tell Mr. Alert who is calling him, please?'

Never say:

'Who is it?'

'What is your name?'

'Sorry, I can't put you through without knowing your name.'

(d) Ask the caller to spell his name, if necessary. The correct information must be passed on to the ultimate recipient of the call.

(e) Please help us to give good service to callers by not eating, smoking or drinking while on duty. If you begin to eat a piece of cake or to suck a sweet and the telephone rings, you will either have to keep the caller waiting, take the remnants of the food or the sweet out of your mouth or go on eating. It is far better not to begin the cycle.

(f) There will be occasions when the switchboard is very busy. You will feel harassed and, sometimes, irritated by the lack of courtesy shown by some callers, but please try very hard to keep calm at all times. It is better for the telephone to keep ringing than for you to take a call which you cannot adequately service. The best way to keep calm is to smile. That will relax you.

(g) You are being supplied with a departmental chart and a list of names of those members of the staff most likely to receive telephone calls.

(h) Do not take messages. If you cannot contact the individual and there is no one else in the department, ask the caller for his telephone number and tell him that his call will be returned as quickly as possible.

(i) Never screen a call. That is part of the duty of a PA, when acting under instructions from her boss.

(j) It is most important that you service all calls. If a caller prefers to hold on instead of being called back, while you try to contact the executive concerned, advise that caller every thirty seconds that you are still trying to locate the executive. Never leave the caller wondering whether he has been cut off. Also, he may wish to change his mind and ask to be phoned back.

(k) If you know that someone has switched to voicemail always forewarn the caller before you put them through.

(l) If you know that the person being called is out, do offer the option of leaving a voicemail message.

(m) Always remember, there is no substitute for charm. The best way to communicate is to smile. It does come across, even though callers can't see you.

These are basic instructions which can be adjusted to suit the policies of individual companies.

It Applies to Everyone
A book of helpful advice on telephone usage should also be given to members of the staff other than the receptionist. It could be based on the following points:

(a) Bad communication is the cause of many major and minor disputes and problems. Because the telephone is a means of communication, everyone should remember its advantages and disadvantages (both for incoming calls and inter-company calls). One disadvantage is that, while one executive may not visit another in his office, or make a journey to visit a supplier, he will hold lengthy conversations over the telephone, keeping the line engaged and, perhaps, stopping an important customer from contacting the department.

Telephone conversations should always be brief; but brevity does not mean curtness or rudeness. It is unusual to take notes of telephone conversation messages, therefore, instructions over the telephone must be clear and precise so that there is no subsequent misunderstanding.

(b) When the telephone rings in a department, it must be answered immediately. Receptionists become frustrated or bad-tempered if there is no co-operation from office staff and no one bothers to answer a ringing phone.

Members of staff should be told that they are *all* responsible for servicing telephone calls. Everyone is involved in helping to make the company more profitable. Even if someone from another department is the only person available in an office, he or she should take responsibility and *pick* up the receiver.

(c) When answering a call, give the name of the department followed by your own name, e.g.:

'Service Department, this is John Smith.'

But that can sound curt, so always add: 'May I help you?' Do that even if the caller is a colleague, because politeness is contagious.

(d) When you are advised by the receptionist of the name of a caller, the greeting can be made more personal:

'Good morning Mr. Harvey, this is John Smith, Service Department. May I help you?'

(e) Satisfying a customer's needs may involve obtaining information from files or associates, so do remember to service the call. Return to the telephone at frequent intervals to apologise for the delay. If it then becomes obvious that the enquiry cannot be dealt with in a reasonable time, suggest telephoning back later with the information. *Always keep that promise.*

(f) When taking a call for a colleague, avoid saying:

'He'll call you back.' Settle the query yourself if at all possible.

(g) Always advise the receptionist if you leave the building, and tell her when you expect to return. Ensure the voice mail message also indicates when you will return.

(h) Never ask the receptionist to take messages for you.

(i) Never discuss a problem with other office personnel over an open telephone receiver.

(j) Ignore colleagues who try to attract your attention or to interrupt you while you are in conversation with a caller.

Complaints

Every organisation receives complaints, some justified, some not, but all those who complain are convinced that they are in the right. Sometimes they are looking for a confrontation. Unfortunately many companies ignore the fact that a complaint put right can mean a customer is retained. Why spend huge sums on advertising and strive for new business to make up for losses which may have been caused by customers who are dissatisfied and have decided to buy elsewhere? And remember, a customer *will* go elsewhere if he feels that he has a complaint which is not being dealt with fairly.

Don't greet the caller with:
- 'What is your complaint?'
- 'What is wrong.'
- 'What's the trouble?'

Do keep to the standard greeting:
- 'How may I help you?'

Handling Complaints

1. Your company should give clear-cut instructions as to what decisions you may make. A dynamic managing director will give fairly broad discretionary powers, otherwise called *delegation*. Without these powers, a caller will be passed from one person to another, with no one willing to accept the responsibility of taking action. Everything possible must be done to satisfy the customer, and advice should only be sought if the decision you have made is not acceptable to the customer.

2. Listen carefully. Let the caller talk himself out. He may run out of steam, and then he will be more amenable to reason.

3. Never interrupt, however unfair the complaint may be. It is difficult to restrain yourself from saying:
   - 'That isn't right.'
   - 'But we did deliver.'
   - 'The parcel left here perfectly packed.'
   - 'It's the way you washed it.'

   Refrain from comment until you have heard the whole story. Jot down notes, if necessary.

4. Never lose your temper. It will not change the attitude of the caller, and can only result in a dissatisfied customer. It is sometimes difficult to remain calm and customers can often be unfair, but to be successful in business is always difficult.

5. Begin by believing that the customer could be right. This will help you to remain calm. Too many employees on the receiving end of complaints believe that their company is always in the right.

6. Show interest in the complaint. Show sympathy as well, if necessary.

7. If you cannot give an instant decision, explain what action you are taking.
   - 'I am sorry, Mr. Brown, that this has happened. I will check with the accounts department and ring you back.'
   - 'Mrs. Jones, from what you have told me there must be a fault in the product. There will be an immediate investigation, and I'll ring you back.'

8. Having promised action, you must take action. Do not put matters off while you deal with something else. Tackle the problem right away, or there is the risk of it being filed and the customer neglected. If you telephone back quickly, this alone will take some of the

irritation out of the irate customer, even if you can only offer a compromise settlement.

9. If you are in the wrong, apologise quickly and unequivocally.

'I am Sorry, Mr. Johnstone – we have really let you down, and there is no excuse. I cannot blame the computer or a strike; it was a human error. I can only apologise once more and assure you that we shall do our best to see that it will never happen again.'

10. If the customer is obviously in the wrong, then try to save his face.

'Tests have shown, Mr. Smith, that the material was burned, but if I were in your place I might not believe that – I would think that the material was faulty. I am sure you are a very fair-minded person, so may I send you a copy of the report?'

'I don't want a report – I want a new suit.'

'Mr. Smith, I am sure you will agree that there is no point in seeking expert advice if it is going to be ignored. I'll tell you what we'll do: if you would like to send the suit to an independent research laboratory for testing, we'll pay the fee if we are proven wrong. Is that reasonable?'

'Well – yes – I suppose so . . .'

'Look Mr. Smith, let's settle the matter while we're on the telephone. We will repair it for you, free of charge. That's fair, isn't it?'

When dealing with a complaint, the aim must always be to *settle it quickly to the satisfaction of the customer.*

The Personal Assistant

Good Personal Assistants are hard to find, and, once found, they should be treasured. The good PA will be able to make decisions, know the boss's plans, thoroughly understand the business and be able to handle people. There are, however, many office workers who could be very good PAs if their responsibilities were recognised and they received training instead of reprimands when things go wrong.

Most executives find it infuriating to receive incorrect telephone messages, or to be given the wrong names of callers.

All executives must keep their PAs advised as to their comings and goings, and never fix appointments without telling their PAs. Without this information, a PA cannot deal effectively or honestly with incoming calls.

Never say any of the following:
- 'He's at a conference.'
- 'I never know where he is.'
- 'He was here a few minutes ago.
- 'I think he'll be back by four. Who is this?'

No one ever believes the last statement, even if it is true. If possible, when callers cannot be connected with the manager, the PA should simply tell the truth:
- 'He's with the plant manager at a meeting.'
- 'He's with a customer in the showroom.'
- 'He's just left for the factory.'
- 'He's with our Dutch agent.'

If a caller is holding on the line until an executive is free, the PA must service the call. She must indicate, at regular intervals, how long she thinks it will be before her manager is free.

A good PA makes certain that her manager is the correct executive to deal with the call. Often, customers and suppliers telephone an executive because they know him personally, or because they want to speak to the top person, when it can just as easily be dealt with by someone else.

The PA must not say, 'What are you calling about?' but she can say:

'He's on the other line at the moment, Mr. Harris – (pause) is this to do with accounts (or sales, delivery, advertising, etc.).'

Even if the PA has made a wrong guess, the caller will nearly always correct her and explain the reason for his call. The PA can then say, 'To save you holding on, Mr. Harris, I think it would be better for me to put you through to Mr. Parsons. He will be able to help you right away.'

A PA will always remember that her courtesy and efficiency on the telephone will reflect on her manager and also on the image of the company.

Make the caller feel welcome, even if you know that he is a miserable curmudgeon who is always complaining. Say:

– 'Oh Mr. Clark, I'm so sorry, but Ms. Best is on holiday. May I help you?'
– 'Mr. Willis, I'm so sorry, but Mr. Williams is at our Dunstable factory. Mrs. Clifford is here, would you like to speak to her?'

Whenever possible, a PA should have the authority to fix an appointment without continually referring back to her manager. She should be in charge of his diary, and know when he is free. This saves endless telephone calls and rescheduling.

A PA must identify her department, name and position as soon as she picks up the receiver.

'This is Mr. Brown's PA, Mrs. Lincoln, speaking. May I help you?'

If a message has to be taken, remember the mnemonic:

> who
> what
> when
> which

- Record *who* the caller is (name, address and telephone number).
- Record *what* she wants (details of message).
- Record *when* action was promised (return call, meeting, appointment, etc.).
- Record *which* facts must be known by the manager before the matter may be settled.

If a PA has to transfer a call, she must *never* say:

'Oh, you want Mr. Jones.'

or:

'You have the wrong person; I'll put you through to Mr. Jones.'

She should say:

'I'm sorry, you have the sales office. May I transfer you to Mr. Jones in the accounts department?'

Enquiries

Staff trained to handle telephone enquiries can turn a high percentage of such calls into orders. Without training, the following scenario is liable to happen:

'Is that the sales office?'

'Yes.'

'I saw your advertisement for the new Denlon shirt, but I can't get any.'

'Where is your shop?'

'I haven't got a shop . . .'

'I'm sorry, but we only supply through retail outlets.'

'I'm not asking you to supply me. I saw your advertisement yesterday. I went to three shops in the Victoria area, but none of them stocks your make. I'm telephoning to find out where I can get one.'

'Hold on.'

A pause. Someone else arrives on the telephone.

'May I help you?'

'I've just explained to your colleague that I want to buy one of your shirts advertised yesterday – the Denlon . . .'

'Selfridge's stock them.'

'But Selfridge's is in Oxford Street, and I'm in Victoria. Isn't there anyone nearer here?'

'Hold on.'

Three minutes later.

'Are you there?'

'Yes.'

'Bakers of William Street have them in stock.'

'But that's one of the shops I went to, and they haven't even heard of your shirt.'

'Well, I suggest you try Selfridge's . . .'

Unfortunately, poorly trained staff mean that scenarios such as this are all too common. Telephone any manufacturer or distributor and make a sales enquiry. The odds are something like twenty to one that you won't get the right answer first time.

Although helpful advice should be given to the receptionist and staff generally, to enable them to handle incoming calls, training must be given to all members of the staff likely to deal with enquiries. This applies equally to the junior recruit and the most senior member of the sales office. All personnel must be kept regularly informed about sales promotions. So often advertisements appear, or direct mail shots are sent out and, with the exception of the salespeople and a selected few, the rest of the office staff are left in the dark. That is the main reason for the caller hearing:

'Hold on . . .'

'What did you say it was?'

'Where did you see it?'

'Are you sure you have the right company?'

There must be preparation. Brochures, advertisement cut-outs, stock lists, colour charts, order packs, price lists, product changes, etc., should be made available to all office staff.

Enquiries are usually answered by a sales manager, assistant sales manager, sales office manager, or senior member of the office staff.

When someone enquires about a product or service, the receptionist will transfer the call to the appropriate person. The snag arises when that person is not in his office and the call is then transferred to the general office, the receptionist hoping that someone will be able to handle it. If properly trained in the technique of handling enquiries, any member of staff should be able to deal with them in one of the following ways:

(a) Give all the facts required.

(b) Give facts, and arrange for a salesperson to call.

(c) Ask for the telephone number so that the sales executive may call back, and say:

'Mr. Jones, I know Ms. Smith, our sales manager, would want to talk to you personally. May she call you back?'

The person accepting the enquiries will identify himself and, by the tone of his voice, show that he is interested and keen for the business. If this is left until all the information has been given, the caller may ring off hastily, saying:

'Thank you very much, that's all I want to know.'

Training must be given in product benefits, so that staff members can close an order or make an appointment for a salesperson to call.

This is how *not* to do it:

'I want a few details of your fire extinguishers. I'm afraid I'm not very technical. Is it easy to operate?'
'Very easy, Mr. Sparks. May I send a salesperson to demonstrate it to you?'
'Not for the time being . . .'

That office junior made no attempt to sell the product. He considered that he had fulfilled his task by telling the caller that the extinguisher was easy to operate, and by suggesting that a salesperson should call.

However, when an enquiry is made, an extra benefit must be stressed. Let us deal with the enquiry again:

'I want a few details of your fire extinguishers. I'm afraid I'm not very technical. Is it easy to operate?'
'First of all, thank you for calling, Mr. Sparks. Your address is?'
'Main Stores, Clark Street, W.1.'
'Thank you, Mr. Sparks. By the way, do you have female employees?'
'Yes, three women.'
'Then you will be happy to know that our Model A extinguisher only weighs four pounds. It is as easy to handle as a small portable radio. Your smallest assistant could pick it up with one hand, easily. But

picking it up isn't everything, Mr. Sparks, is it? You will want to know about the operation.'

'Yes. As I said, we're not very technical here.'

'It's as easy as opening a suitcase. You just flip a catch and press a button. It's as simple as that.'

'It sounds easy enough.'

'And what is more, Mr. Sparks, small as it is, it will put out an average fire in seconds – and, after all, all large fires start with a small fire. I'm sure you will want protection right away, isn't that so, Mr. Sparks?'

'Well – er – yes.'

'Good. Then I suggest that I book an order for one. The price is £80 – and I'll arrange for an expert to call and advise you about siting it. He will also make sure that all your needs are covered.'

An attempt must always be made to close an order on the telephone. The fact that someone has made the enquiry means that they are interested. By selling first, and subsequently arranging an appointment the objection to a salesperson is nearly always overcome. Even if an order cannot be booked over the telephone, the extra benefit of the service or product must still be stressed.

That Extra Service

In business today, there is little to choose between many similar products or services. Whether you are in the office-cleaning field or selling cars, insurance, consumer goods, capital equipment or publishing, you are never so far ahead of your competitors that you can be certain of retaining any of your customers. You have some pluses and some minuses. So have your competitors.

The dynamic company will always get more than its share of the market because it will always try to offer some kind of extra service – an extra service so rarely given by companies, both large and small. That extra service is to make sure that everyone who telephones your company is given a warm and friendly welcome, is dealt with efficiently and courteously, and is made to feel that the call is not an intrusion on someone's time, but a very welcome event.

'How may I help you' must convey the message *I really do want to help you.*

CHAPTER 9

Outgoing Calls

'Mr. Johnstone, I have a call for you. I've tried to contact your PA but he is not in his office.'

'Don't worry. Who wants me?'

'A Mr. Arnold Coopersmith.'

'What does he want?'

Then, suddenly remembering his own rule that the receptionist must not waste time questioning callers, he adds hastily:

'Just put him through.'

'It's his PA, I should think, Mr. Johnstone.'

'Doesn't matter, put her through.'

A pause, then a voice says:

'Is that Mr. Johnstone?'

'Yes.'

'Mr. William Johnstone?'

'Yes.'

'Will you hold on a minute please? I have Mr. Coopersmith for you.'

A minute passes, then:

'I'm sorry, Mr. Johnstone, but Mr. Coopersmith is out of his office. He was there when I made the call, and I'm sure he won't be more than a few seconds . . .'

Johnstone is about to replace the receiver when Mr. Coopersmith comes on the line.

'Mr. Johnstone?'

'Yes.'

'You don't know me, but our mutual friend George Clark told me to call you.'

Something like 20% of executives wanting to make a telephone call ask their PA or receptionist to obtain the person they want to contact. This is *the* unpardonable telephone sin. Whether due to pomposity, thoughtlessness, a wish to show authority to junior staff ('Get me so-and-so on the line'), the pretence of being too busy to dial a number or lack of common courtesy, this practice is a sure way of alienating customers and annoying friends.

A caller, whatever his position in an organisation, must get his own number, either by self-dialling or by asking the receptionist to give him a line. I am referring to calls to customers, although this rule also applies to telephoning many other people.

Sales Calls
Selling over the telephone, other than making appointments, can be divided into two main categories:
(a) *Repeat business*
   Telephone salespeople regularly obtain repeat orders from stores, shops, hospitals, etc., but except for special promotions, they rarely initiate sales over the telephone. Selling to retailers, wholesalers, and direct to the public, is covered in Chapter 10 – *The Telephone Selling Organisation*.
(b) *Specialised Selling*
   This entails closing deals over the telephone for which quotations may have been sent, or direct selling of services or products.

Specialised Selling, Prospecting
Telephone salespeople work from two lists – prospects and past customers. The capital goods salesperson unlike the salesperson of consumer goods and consumer durables, does not have the advantage of running

accounts. He cannot telephone weekly for repeat business. If, for example, he sells an advertising sign to Bright & Company, it is doubtful whether he will be able to sell another sign to Bright & Company for several months, and possibly years. The same would apply to blinds or canopies for shops. Replacements may only be needed every five years or more. Additional vending machines, additional fire extinguishers or voicemail systems cannot be sold on a regular repeat basis, but they can be sold over a period of time. However, the telephone salesperson must still remember to *use his users*. Past customers are better contacts to make than prospects. Customer records must, therefore, always be kept up-to-date and accessible at the appropriate time. Before telephoning a customer, the salesperson will check the records and then work out his hook. It is sub-standard selling to telephone and say:

'I'm sure it is time for you to have another cigarette machine in your canteen.'

'Our Review of Industry is being published on the first of January. Last year you took out a half-page ad. Would you like a full page now in the new issue?'

These approaches could be changed by thinking of a good hook.

(a) *The Window Display Hook*

'Mr. Barker, when I passed your shop on Tuesday, I admired your beautiful display of colourful ceramics. Do you change the display often?'

'Yes, we find it attracts attention.'

'Mr. Barker, because it is so successful, you will want to enhance the colourful display by changing your canopy to one of our new multi-coloured designs. It will line up with any display you make. This means that more passers-by will stop and admire . . .'

(b) *Exhibition Hook*

'Mr. Smith, were you able to visit the Vending Machine Exhibition?'

'No, I couldn't manage it.'

'What a pity: I was looking forward to seeing you again and showing you our new unit with the armour plate glass front, which means that more cigarettes will be sold from it. It is the equivalent of a modern window display. You told me about your canteen extension, but I didn't want to let you have another unit until our new model was on the market. Delivery at the moment is slow, but I will . . .'

(c) *The Concession Hook*

'Ms. Wilson, you will be pleased to know that the new Review of Industry, out in January, can help you in two ways: firstly, circulation is being increased by 10%, but we have not increased our advertising rates; secondly, you can now have a full page facing the copy. This is a special concession to you, Ms. Wilson, as a regular advertiser.'

Plan, Plan, Plan

There is no substitute for pre-call planning. It is the only way to sell effectively. Get the facts, find the hook, pinpoint the main benefit, and close quickly.

Cold Calling

Cold calling, whether by personal calling or telephoning, is never easy. The salesperson who cold calls has to have an extra attribute – strength of character, determination, perseverance – call it what you will, but it means the toughness to accept many 'no's' to obtain just one 'yes'.

The telephone saleperson with the wrong mental

attitude curses his luck at being in a job in which so many calls are wasted. Soon, he is demoralised. The professional telephone salesperson believes that every call is profitable; it is only a question of averaging. He looks at it this way: if an order is worth £500 and he has had to take nine 'no's' before getting a 'yes' on the tenth call, then every call has earned him £50. That is the right mental attitude.

Remember, I am now referring to selling direct on the telephone, not to obtaining appointments, which is much easier.

Planning for Cold Calls

First must come the perfection of a sales presentation, and then a further study of the market. What is the best time to telephone a prospect? This can vary from business to business, and it is not possible to lay down a hard and fast rule. Every telephone salesperson must carry out her own market research. For example, there is rarely a time when someone with a large family is completely free from duties, but you may find that after the person finishes shopping and taking the children to school, about eleven o'clock in the morning, is the ideal time for an approach from you.

Only continual research on the part of a telephone salesperson will help her to cut out time-wasting calls. Some telephone salesperson will be able to work all day, while others may only be able to work for two hours in the morning and evening, depending on the type of prospect they are contacting.

The aim is to make as many calls as possible. That is why the rule for the teleseller is that after she hears six rings on the telephone and there is no reply, she should cut off and try someone else. Time is vital.

Many telephone salespeople find that store buyers may be contacted more easily between 4–5 p.m. than before 11 a.m. when they are seeing representatives. Doctors, on the other hand, are best telephoned before they start their morning rounds or just after the evening surgery. Between 7.30–8.30 a.m. has been found to be a good time to contact top executives, while the owners of retail shops prefer to be called before 9.30 a.m. or early in the afternoon before people who aren't working in offices return to shopping after lunch.

No telephone salesperson, however, can work rigidly to a timetable. He must believe that his products or services are so excellent that the prospect will want to speak to him whenever he calls. By providing himself with a work pattern, however, he will be able to concentrate his efforts during those times when his calls will be best received.

Set Targets

When selling direct, you must set yourself a daily target and never sell yourself short. There can be many excuses for ending a telephone call:

– 'Not feeling too well.'
– 'Everyone's busy at this time of the year.'
– 'No one wants a phone call while there's a strike on.'
– 'It doesn't seem to be my lucky day.'

If every author who sets himself a daily target, stopped because he lacked inspiration or had a headache or wanted to go for a stroll, few books would ever be written. The teleseller, like the author, creates, because a sales presentation is a creation, and he hopes to close his story with a happy ending – that is, an order.

Set yourself a target, and keep to it.

Leads

The life blood of the telephone salesperson is leads. She will use websites, classified directories, business registers, trade journals, house magazines, newspaper advertisements, estate agents and chambers of commerce. She will also observe and note down new shops opening, changes of occupancy, or a house decoration which is taking place, but her main objective is always to obtain leads.

The successful telephone salesperson is a joiner. She will join clubs and trade organisations. She attends meetings and listens to lectures. She enjoys doing these things, but she also has the objective of obtaining leads. She will say:

– 'It's been nice meeting you. May I give you a ring sometime?'
– 'Do you mind if I ring him and mention your name?'
– 'Perhaps you know of someone interested in . . .'
– 'I'll let you have a copy, and then telephone you.'

Most people like to be helpful. If they are asked for advice, they will readily give it. If asked for leads, they will try to help.

Last thing every evening, the telephone salesperson will prepare her work for the next day. She will not want to waste precious minutes during the morning selling time by *leaving things till tomorrow*. She will prepare a list of contacts for calls to be made. She will also check her presentation.

Are any changes to be made?

What will be the main benefit of each call?

What will she use as a hook?

The hook, to the teleseller selling direct, is just as

important as it is to the salesperson calling on her customers for repeat orders, or trying to obtain appointments by telephone.

With some prospects, she may use the 'letter hook' – with others, the 'recommendation hook' or the 'special offer hook'.

The cold caller must keep to the rules:

(a) Careful preparation
(b) The right presentation
(c) The right hook
(d) The right prospect list
(e) The right main benefit
(f) The right mental attitude.

SERVICING CUSTOMERS

It is less expensive to service existing customers over the telephone than by personal calling. The larger companies in the consumer field have their own telephone sales division. This aspect of telephone usage is covered in Chapter 10, *The Telephone Selling Organisation*, but companies in every market will find it well worthwhile to maintain good customer relations by better use of the telephone.

The formula is simple:

1. Use the buyer's name
2. Identify yourself
3. Give benefits of new products and new promotions
4. Thank the buyer, and indicate when you will telephone again.

REVIVING INACTIVE ACCOUNTS

A buyer will never object to a telephone call expressing concern at not receiving his business. All inactive accounts should be telephoned.

'Good morning, Mrs. Bristow, this is Tony Thorpe of Cray Brothers. The manager of our order department has told me that we haven't had an order from you for three months. This concerns us deeply, and I am telephoning to find out the reason for this, Mrs. Bristow.'

ADVANCE INFORMATION

A sales journey time might be six weeks, or a salesperson may only make a visit three times a year. This leaves room for a competitor to take away business. A good way of keeping customers loyal is to use the telephone to advise them of new advertising programmes, TV features, new products, new designs, new technical factors, etc. You could say, for example:

'Mr. Leslie, I am telephoning you specially because I wanted you to know about a new feature of our unit which will be on the market next month.'

or

'Ms. Wise, you will shortly be receiving full details of our dynamic new TV advertising campaign, which will bring you a lot of business. I wanted you to be one of the first to know our plans.'

REPLYING TO LETTERS

A shortage of staff is often used as an excuse for the delay in replying to a letter. Some firms think it sufficient if a brief, almost curt, acknowledgement is sent. How much better it is to telephone, whenever possible. This action saves time, pleases customers, and can even cut costs.

When an enquiry is received through the post, many sales executives dictate letters which may be typed a day or so later. Precious days are lost before the prospect receives the information he is seeking. A telephone call could be much more effective in helping to capture an order while a competitor is still dictating her mail.

Letters of Complaint
Whenever letters of complaint are received, it is important that they are dealt with quickly. Nothing eases a delicate situation more than for a customer to receive a telephone call offering him an apology or an explanation.

However well a letter is written in response to a complaint, there is always the possibility of it being misunderstood. Also, from the time the complaint letter is written until a reply is sent could be seven days. This could turn a simmering customer into a boiling-point customer.

Whenever possible, a letter of complaint should be dealt with immediately by telephone. The way to handle the complaint is covered in Chapter 8, *Incoming Calls*, but your approach will be different in each situation.

First, there are some rules which must be adhered to:

1. Make sure the letter is fully understood.

2. Find out the facts of the case.
3. List all the points you wish to raise with the customer.
4. When making the call, restate the salient features of the letter.
5. Answer the complaint fully and effectively.
6. Make certain that the customer is satisfied with the explanations given, and the action to be taken.

You must now consider what your approach will be. You might say:

– 'Mr. Curtis, I have just received your letter and I must apologise right away for what has happened.'
– 'Ms. Brown, I have just received your letter and if I were in your shoes I would be feeling just as you do.'
– 'Mr. Smith, I have only just received your letter and I cannot make any excuses for the lateness of our delivery to you. I can only offer you an explanation.'
– 'Mrs. Jones, I have just received your letter and I am so sorry to hear of your complaint. I am sure that, as a fair-minded person, you will want to briefly hear our side of the story.'

Whether you are in the right or wrong, always begin with an apology. Even if you are in the right, there must have been some misunderstanding for the customer to write a letter of complaint.

COLLECTING ACCOUNTS

Every efficient company is tightening its credit control. An adequate cash flow is all important and, to maintain it, every effort must be made to ensure that debtors settle their accounts as quickly as possible.

A collection policy might be that all accounts one month overdue will be threatened with legal proceedings. If the account is not settled within the next seven days, court action is taken. This could bring in the cash, but it could also lose customers.

No marketing director would accept a policy of continually threatening action against good customers who could always place large orders elsewhere. These days, a credit controller has to work closely with the marketing team, although the credit controller must have the final decision as to whether or not an account should be closed.

Most credit controllers would have less worries if they used the telephone more efficiently for debt collection.

Letters, however well written, do not influence the hard core of slow payers, and are thrown into the waste paper basket by those not afraid of legal threats. The weakness of a letter is that it is frequently not per-sonalised. So, a letter might seem fair-minded and kindly to the writer, but may be read by the recipient as a curt, blunt demand for payment.

Companies have thousands of accounts, so letters and reminders will still have to be written, and only a selected few can be dealt with by telephone. But most credit controllers can use the telephone with great success. The majority of people pay up more readily when spoken to in an understanding manner over the telephone.

But the accounts collector must remind herself constantly that:

1. Account collection by telephone can only succeed if staff are trained in telephone technique. It is better to write letters than to allow untrained personnel loose on the telephone.

2. The collector must talk to the person who can pass the account for payment. It is no use having messages passed on.

3. She must not be put off by elusive debtors. She must keep on telephoning. The debtor, unless he does not mind his whole staff knowing that he is being pressed for payment, will eventually speak on the telephone. If he is very troublesome, one of his assistants should be asked for his private telephone number. He or she may not provide it, but the debtor will get the message.

4. The salesperson must know exactly what she is going to say, and have all the relevant details in front of her before she dials the number.

5. She must set up a definite procedure. For example, telephone calls might be made 21 days after statements have been submitted. If these rules are adhered to, debtors will accept the calls as being part of normal business procedure.

6. There must be a close to the sale – because it is a sale. The collector has to influence the debtor to take action against his wishes. The close would be a promise to pay in full, to pay something on account, to send a cheque by return, or to give a definite date when a cheque will be sent.

7. The collector's job is to collect the accounts *and* to keep the customer's goodwill.

Problems and Solutions
The credit control manager faces many problems. In the main, these will fall into the following categories:

White & Co.	Good customers, policy is to take long credit.
Black & Co.	Good customers, temporarily short of cash.

Green & Co.	Living on knife-edge and paying those suppliers first who worry them the most.
Blue & Co.	Customer who refuses to settle accounts because of a grievance.
Red & Co.	Good customer, but sometimes bad payer. A stop has to be placed on the dispatch of goods to them.

1. *White & Co.*

The accountant of White & Co. is not influenced by threats. Threatening will bring about the closing of the account, unless White's buyer insists on having the products. But few buyers stand their ground when faced with a policy of obtaining long credit which may have been laid down by top management.

White's accountant will ignore standard letters and even pleading letters, but regular telephoning can change the situation dramatically. A friendly relationship must be developed with him, and his help sought rather than demands made.

Your approach should be:

'We are both doing our job, and we should help each other.'

If the demands are reasonable, they will be met. The aim must be to extract a promise from the accountant every time he is telephoned.

The *Whites* of the business world have the cash, but want to make use of yours. Don't let them do it. They are usually proud of their integrity and standing, and they expect others to be humbled by their size and reputation. They can always pay if they want to.

Telephoning *White & Co.* is not a job for a junior. The

aim is to get on first-name terms with whoever is in authority at *White's* and can sign a cheque or sanction payment. If this rapport is built up, payment will be made to you while others are sending out letters, begging, pleading, or even whining for their money.

2. *Black & Co.*

There is always a debtor pattern. Usually, *Black & Co.* pays up promptly and that is why it is disconcerting when they begin to take long credit. *Black & Co.*, unlike *White & Co.*, have never made it their policy to make use of suppliers' credit to help finance their business, but while they may have had a successful year last year, during the current year, profits may have dropped. If a bad year's trading follows a successful year, the taxes from the good year are payable at a time when trading and cash flow may be at a low ebb. This could be one reason why *Black & Co.* are temporarily short of money. It could be that they have heavy capital commitments, or have made a large bad debt. The reason for their slow payment should be discovered if possible. A check at Companies House will give some indication of the position, but the accounts will not be up-to-date. If it is believed that *Black & Co.* are only temporarily short of cash, then the credit controller, when telephoning, should use the *Question* technique:

> 'Mr. Black, I always look upon your company as one of our most regular payers of accounts. Is there any reason why you are now withholding payment?'
>
> Mr. Black will probably tell the truth, and the credit controller should then make a reasonable proposal:
>
> 'Mr. Black, you don't want me telephoning you every month. If we give you X days of extra credit, will you meet our account promptly?'

If the *Mr. Blacks* of this world make a promise to keep to a new arrangement, they will keep to it.

3. *Green & Co.*

A credit controller will quickly place *Green & Co.* in the right category and will, therefore, make a rule that they must be telephoned within seven days of receiving statements, although the account may not really be overdue.

It must be made plain to *Mr. Green* that extended credit cannot be given. A promise must be extracted from him, and that promise must be payment by return. If it is not received, another telephone call must be made – daily calls, if necessary. This is the only way to get *Green* to pay without taking legal action.

4. *Blue & Co.*

These are the customers to be handled with kid gloves. Before telephoning *Blue*, a careful check should be made to discover if there is any grievance. Many customers withhold payments, sometimes unfairly, because goods are unsatisfactory, service poor, or a salesperson's promise has not been kept. Sometimes the grievance is not known. If it is suspected, the credit controller should say:

'Mr. Blue, you are one of our most valued customers. There must be a reason for your withholding payment. Please tell me what it is so that I can put matters right immediately.'

If there is any correspondence in the file, it will often be found that promises have been made by salespeople which have not been kept. A promise must be extracted from *Mr. Blue* to send a cheque off immediately on the understanding that the matter will be investigated and put right. Also, the salesperson concerned must be made to call on him within twenty-four hours to offer his apologies.

5. *Red & Co.*
The salesperson must not be instructed to take the matter up with *Red & Co.'s* buyer. This can only cause friction between the buyer and the salesperson, resulting in loss of goodwill.

Red's accounts manager should be telephoned.

'Mr. Smith, obviously your buyer does not know of our credit arrangements, and he has placed another order with us while the previous account is overdue. If you will send a cheque off today, I will release the goods immediately so that your buyer will not be short of stock. I am sure you would want that, wouldn't you, Mr. Smith?'

Save His Face

Telephoning, then, is an effective system of collecting accounts. It can be less expensive than the cost of writing letters, and it gets results.

The telephone accounts collector must remember:

1. To be tactful.
2. He must not discuss the debt with junior members of the debtor's staff.
3. He must use such sentences as:
   'We are all in the same boat these days.'
   'You are one of our best accounts.'
   'We are also telephoned for payment. It's a vicious circle, and we must all help each other.'
   'You have such a fine reputation for paying promptly.'
   'I know I can rely on you.'

4. He must keep his temper, however rude or ill-tempered the debtor may be.

An efficient telephone collecting service can not only improve a cash flow and reduce bad debts, but it can also help to increase business.

CHAPTER 10

The Telephone Selling Organisation

There are four fields of activity in which large scale telephone selling can operate. They are:

(a) Manufacturers and wholesalers in food distribution, selling to retailers and caterers.
(b) Newspapers selling classified advertisements and, to a lesser extent, magazines and trade journals selling advertising space or subscriptions.
(c) Retail stores receiving incoming calls from customers and selling direct to their customers.
(d) Telephone selling contractors retained by companies on a fee or a contract basis to carry out campaigns.

Although, in this chapter, we study the telephone structure of two large organisations, its principles can easily be adapted to the setting up and functioning of a small division of only two or three telesales staff.

The Telephone Selling Manager

A typical structure of marketing management is shown overleaf.

Although the marketing director is ultimately responsible for the successful launching of his company's products or services, it is the sales manager who will augment the sales on a day-to-day basis. Regional managers under his control will supervise their areas, but the telephone sales manager will control all of the teams selling by telephone throughout the country. She will appoint supervisors and engage, train and motivate staff.

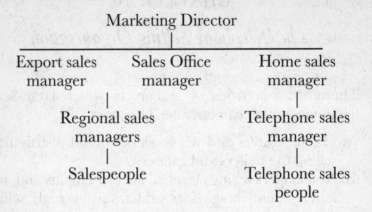

Profile of a Telephone Sales Manager
The Telephone Sales Managers I met when re-searching for this book had many characteristics in common. Before commencing telephone selling, their backgrounds were:

(a) property negotiator
(b) assistant in a department store
(c) cosmetic representative
(d) telephone receptionist
(e) store demonstrator of electrical appliances
(f) secretary
(g) ladies' wear representative.

One common factor was experience in selling or dealing with the public before becoming telephone sales people and subsequently achieving promotion. It would seem from this evidence that, although many highly efficient telephone sales people have no sales background, this experience is advantageous if promotion is to be achieved.

The other common factors were:

(a) dedication to work. Three of them are married; the others are single. They are prepared to talk about telephone selling all of the working day, but married people claim that they drop the subject on returning home in the evenings.
(b) They are bright, lively and smart people and set a fine example to their staff in dress and appearance.
(c) They are all articulate.
(d) They know how to get along with people.

When seeking a telephone manager, therefore, one should look for an articulate, sincere and understanding person.

It is not possible to build a successful telephone sales department without having a highly competent person in control, fully backed by a director.

The Sales Team

All companies use similar procedures for engaging staff. A few years ago, advertisements for telephone selling staff were strictly formal, as:

EXCELLENT OPPORTUNITY TO
JOIN TELEPHONE SELLING TEAM

or, just simply:

TELEPHONE SALES STAFF REQUIRED

This has changed. Executives have caught up with the idea that advertisements must be attractive to applicants. They must have YOU appeal, and list many benefits.

Here is one:

JOIN A HAPPY TEAM

Our telephone sales people have the opportunity of

earning well above average incomes, winning prizes (a trip abroad is not unusual), building a really worthwhile career, and being happy in their work . . .

Here is a gimmicky advertisement:

TELESELL FOR BELLE

You may not be called Belle, but if you like using the telephone, have a pleasant voice and like working with a happy team, you should call us right away. You might be just the Belle for us, which will mean, for you, a good salary . . .

Here is a team-appeal advertisement:

JOIN US

Emma was once a secretary, Paul a model, and Carol an hotel receptionist. Emma, Paul and Carol are now highly successful in telephone sales. Not only do they achieve a high reward for their efforts, but their work is stimulating, challenging and interesting. If you would like to join us . . .

And this is a challenge advertisement:

YOU?

Have you a sparkling personality and the determination to earn the highest possible salary? You have? Good! If you have an attractive voice and like working with a happy team . . .'

Although approximately 90% of telephone sales staff are found through advertisements, the balance of 10% is recommended by friends employed by the company. If the average is below 10%, the manager should take a close look into the conditions under which staff work, and discover if they are really happy in their telephone selling.

But even with the near ideal telephone sales organisation, staff turnover is still heavy, for the usual reasons. Some are only seeking temporary work before going abroad or on holiday, others have babies, or a partner has to move to a new area because of work. Because of this, a telephone manager should try to build up a reserve list of potential employees. Advertising means delays and, if there is a waiting list, vacancies can be filled much more quickly.

Most managers agree on the personality profile most likely to succeed in the job:

Sociable.   Has other interests and a wide circle of friends.

Courteous.   It is easy to tell whether someone is courteous when they telephone for the vacancy, or attend the interview.

Endurance.   It can be gruelling, selling over the telephone, hour after hour.

The background of the applicant, how many jobs someone has already held, family, and so on, will all give some indication of endurance potential.

Voice clarity can be tested over the telephone, and temperament discovered by questioning. A temperamental person will never succeed in telephone selling.

The following case studies will show how the objective of finding the right person, training and managing them are put into practice.

SMEDLEY ROSS FOODS LTD.

This company markets a wide range of canned and frozen foods through wholesale and retail channels and direct to caterers.

The work of the telesales staff is mainly concerned with frozen foods. A few of this company's well-known products are fish fingers, beefburgers, crinkle cut chips and cod steaks.

The manager of the telephone selling operation is Rosemary McColl. The following is a summary of one of our meetings:

'What is your title, Rosemary?'

'National Telephone Sales Supervisor.

'And what are your responsibilities?'

'Briefly, the engaging, training, and motivating of telephone sales people.'

'You cover the whole of the country, which must mean that you travel a great deal.'

'Nearly all the time. I have to cover fifty depots.'

'The depots being, in the main, warehouses from which the stock is delivered?'

'Yes, and each one has its own telephone sales team.'

'Would you like to tell me how the team is made up?'

'The average number of people for a telephone selling area is six, including a supervisor. Each works closely with a salesperson in the field.'

'Do they sell only to retailers?'

'No, usually three telesales and three field salespeople sell to retailers and the same number sell to caterers.'

'How are the telesales staff paid?'

'Salary, plus a weekly bonus. But there are other incentives. We hold regular competitions in which both the salespeople and their telephone selling partners take part. Prizes have included clothes, watches, even a holiday abroad.'

'Obviously, by offering joint prizes you create a team spirit, and you also obviate friction which might occur if one person got a prize and another didn't, as they are both concentrating on the same customers. But there must be friction, surely?'

Rosemary shook her head. She answered:

'No, they really do work in harmony, with the aim of giving a good service to our customers.'

'The accent in the consumer field is, of course, on service?'

'Definitely. If we sell persuasively, it is because we know that the retailer will leave himself short if we don't ask him to increase his order, when necessary.'

'What do you mean by selling persuasively?'

'We may have a special promotion and a retailer may usually take a dozen of a product, but a salesperson will say, "I will send you two dozen." She doesn't ask what he wants because she knows what he can sell. That is why the liaison between telesales and field sales is so important. Salespeople, of course, often know retailers' stocks and potential sales better than retailers do themselves,'

'Tell me how telesales staff manage to work so closely with the field sales staff without having orders duplicated, or telephoning just after the salesperson has left.'

'It's all very simple. The salesperson visits his depot once a week, but he telephones his selling partner at least three times a day for a joint check. You see, the salesperson will only call on a retailer approximately every three weeks, depending on the retailer's turnover, but the telesales person will call the retailer once a week, or in the case of a supermarket, once a day.'

'Do telesales staff find that the retailer is sometimes too busy to speak to them when they call?'

'No, he knows the time of day of each call and is prepared for it. Very quickly a friendly relationship is established between our staff and the retailers. The customers nearly always use our sales people's first names.'

'How many calls do they make each day?'

'Between 60 and 70.'

'How are they kept up-to-date about your regular promotions?'

'We have monthly promotions, and these are explained to both internal and external staff at a meeting attended by the advertising manager and the regional manager. The meetings are held in a local hotel at about 4.30 in the afternoon. Also, newsletters are sent out regularly, coupled with an updated presentation guide.'

'You have about three hundred lines in your range. How do you sell them to caterers?'

'They are divided under twelve headings, and telesales staff present a case, usually dealing with one product under each heading. They could not possibly sell the whole range, but when they know that there is a special need for a product, they persuade the caterer to agree to an appointment for one of our cookery experts to call.'

'How do you recruit?'

'Mostly by local advertising, but we are very selective. I find I have to interview about fifteen people to engage one.'

'What training do you give them?'

'We hold a week-long course. We begin by providing company knowledge, then spend two days on product knowledge and invoicing procedures. The rest of the time is divided into dealing with objections, co-operating with salespeople, a question session, and sales presentation.'

'You do provide them with a sales presentation, then?'

'For special promotions, we give guidelines, but we do explain that every call must use the standard formula:

   Contact and Approach
   Interest
   Product
   Close.'

'Do demonstrations take place, or role-playing?'

'Oh yes, we have many two-way telephone conversations, with a training supervisor or myself acting as a customer, either retailer or caterer. Sometimes we make calls to the sales trainees and other times they originate the calls to us.

'Do your sales people both originate calls, then, and accept in-coming calls?'

'Yes. I know that in some organisations, different teams each have a special function, but we find that in our call centre it is quite easy to allocate incoming calls to the staff who are free at any particular moment.'

'Finally, do you have standard approaches?'

'Yes, for example, we never say to a retailer, "I am calling to find out what you need", but, "I am calling you about tomorrow's delivery."'

Smedley Ross Foods Ltd., have a highly efficient telephone selling operation controlled by a highly efficient national sales supervisor.

THE EVENING STANDARD

This London newspaper's classified advertisement department was once the *most modern and rapidly expanding one in Western Europe*, with the *most intensive training in the country*.

Although today their training methods probably have changed, judging from what I saw of their Telephone Sales Division and the results which this division achieved, they were certainly most efficient, and the department seethed with activity.

The controller was a woman who had the title of Group Tele/Ad Manager. She explained with great enthusiasm how her staff had helped to build the advertising pages of the *Evening Standard*.

I asked her what criteria she set when engaging staff. She answered:

'When an applicant telephones, the person has to sound like a nice person to get an interview. We work as a team here and, however good an applicant might be, I want to be certain that a new employee will fit in well with the other staff members.'

'But you want previous experience?'

'Not really. We employ an ex-model, an ex-actor, an ex-secretary – in fact, ex-almost everything. If someone is an enthusiast and has a good speaking voice, we can train them to succeed.'

'What training do you give?'

'The initial training period lasts a week, but there is continual refresher training.'

'Can you give me some idea of the induction training course?'

'I like to build morale from the beginning, so first we tell them why they have been specially chosen for the job, why they have succeeded where others have failed and, of course, we have to tell them about us – the newspaper industry generally, and classified advertising in particular – and the way we work. We explain the overall market and, of course, cover administration. Next comes one of the most important sessions: *How to Write Advertising Copy.*'

'You manage to do all that in a week?' I asked.

'Yes,' she answered, 'there is no mystique about copy writing – only common sense. It isn't difficult; it is quite simple to change an advertisement which is uninteresting into one which sparkles. We want our advertisers to use copy which gives results, and therefore, if their copy is not good enough, we have to help them. We instil in our staff pride in their job, and their main objective is to help advertisers to achieve results, so that they give us more business.'

'Do you teach them a sales sequence during the induction course?'

'Most definitely. They have to keep to standard guidelines. Following the *Sequence*, we teach them *How to Answer Objections*, and then we have demonstrations, with myself and one of the supervisors acting the part of the advertisers.'

'You mention that you deal with objections.'

'Yes.'

'I should like to ask you how your staff deal with one particular objection. You teach them how to increase an order for a single insertion into a series of four, on the understanding that the advertiser can cancel any of the remaining advertisements after the initial one has appeared, if he or she has obtained satisfactory results. Also, you offer a fifth insertion free of charge, if the results from the first four have not been good enough. Am I right?'

'Yes.'

'Firstly, why do you make this offer?'

'To help the advertiser. If only one insertion is taken and it is not able to bring results – and no single advertisement can be guaranteed to bring in the required replies – then the advertiser is dissatisfied with the newspaper and he has also wasted a considerable amount of time and money. By offering the additional advertisements with a cancellation clause – and we accept the cancellation without question – the advertiser will almost certainly obtain the results he wants.'

'Fair enough. So now for my objection: I have accepted your offer of a series, but I shan't have the replies to the first insertion and be able to evaluate them before the others appear. If I use a box number, there is an even greater delay so, whatever happens, it looks as though I am going to be stuck with the four advertisements. Surely it would be better for me to put them in one at a time with a period in between?'

'I don't agree, Mr. Tack. What are you advertising for – or pretending to advertise for?'

'We'll say a secretary.'

'And you want the best available.'

'Of course.'

'And, as a good business man, you will want to see a number of applicants so that you can make certain of selecting the right person for the job.'

'Yes.'

'And you want to fill the vacancy quickly.'

'Yes.'

'Then, Mr. Tack, that is the very reason why you should take a series, so that you will be certain of obtaining a sufficient number of replies from which you can select your short list.'

I laughed, and said, 'I'm sold.'

'We also teach them,' she said, 'that, if it is necessary, they should suggest having two or three days between the first and second advertisements, so that the objection you raised is overcome.'

'They are taught copy writing, a sales sequence, and how to answer objections. What else?'

'We like them to suggest ideas for the layout of an advertisement – for example, semi-display when necessary. A good headline can also attract attention.'

'May I hear some of your team at work now?'

'Of course.'

I was taken, then, on a conducted tour of the department, and listened to several of the salespeople selling.

There were three sections, each controlled by a supervisor. The switchboard technology automatically searched for a free line, so that the caller was kept on the line no longer than necessary and the staff, therefore, were continually occupied in selling. There were nine people in each team. Some handled incoming calls only; others cold canvassed for advertisements. There was also a person who took orders for cancellations, or changes in advertisements.

I asked the Group Tele/Ad Manager how the salespeople canvassing for orders obtained their prospect lists.

'Each morning, they are given cuttings from the previous day's newspapers or magazines, and these provide good leads. We also give them prospect lists which show the names of previous advertisers, such as car showrooms, restaurants, cinemas, etc.'

'How do they approach someone who has advertised in another newspaper?'

'Firstly, they never ask if the advertiser is satisfied with results. They are taught the subsidiary question technique. Listen now to Joan . . .'

I listened to a sale being made by Joan (I have changed the name of the salesperson and the customer):

'Mr. Johnson, it's Joan Sims of the *Evening Standard* Classified Advertisement Department. You advertised your car in yesterday's –'

'Yes.'

'Is it a blue car, Mr. Johnson?'

'No, red.'

'Does it have a stereo?'

'Yes, quite a good one.'

'How about the tyres – are they in good condition?'

'Excellent condition.'

'Has it anti-lock brakes?'

'Yes.'

The questioning went on for only a few seconds, and Mr. Johnson was obviously deeply interested, because Joan was talking about *his* car and *his* interests.

Quickly, she tied up the deal by suggesting an entirely different wording to the advertisement he had used before – one which highlighted all the car's main features.

Mr. Johnson said, 'I think it's worth a hundred pounds more for all that. What do you think?'

'I think you're right,' Joan said, and the order was clinched.

Next, I heard a good sale to a car dealer who had not advertised for a week or two in the paper. His reason was:

'I'm short of stock, so why should I advertise?'

'That sounds reasonable, Mr. Smith. I suggest you advertise for second-hand cars to give you some cars to sell.'

Mr. Smith laughed.

'It isn't as bad as all that.'

'Have you a red one in stock, Mr. Smith?'

'No, only a metallic blue one.'

It was the questioning technique again, and finally Mr. Smith agreed not only to advertise the blue car, but also one or two others that he suddenly found he had in stock.

The message from the Group Tele/Ad Manager was loud and clear: the success of a telephone selling department stems from the work of the manager, who must be backed by a director. When the manager, in turn, handpicks a good team, inspires and enthuses them, then they must succeed.

The overall need, however, is for the controller to be someone who is dedicated to the work of the division.

It is easy to find consultants who will advise on the equipment and technology needed. But, without someone in charge who can maintain enthusiasm by continual training and inspiration, the equipment and the planning can never be used to best effect.

CHAPTER 11

Buyers Can be Difficult

Sometimes buyers are predictable, and, at other times, unpredictable. The nervous buyer will always be nervous. The chatty buyer will always want to waste time talking about everything except placing an order.

Their attitudes, therefore, to telephone salespeople, are understood from the moment the approach is made. But the unpredictable buyer may change in mood or attitude as readily as a chameleon changes colour – friendly one moment, bad-tempered the next. One chance remark can bring about this change. A seemingly polite person can become four-letter rude if he feels that he is being talked down to, or that a complaint he is making is being minimised. At times, therefore, all buyers are easy to sell to, and at other times they can prove to be most difficult.

We cannot change people, but what we can do is to recognise their strengths and weaknesses, their emotions and temperaments, so that we can help them to come to a decision in our favour. Success in all forms of selling depends on our ability to motivate people. We can best do this when we can communicate with them in such a way that we can allay their fears, soothe their tempers, or feed their egos – in other words, when we know how to handle them.

The Logical Buyer
The logical buyer is a person with a clear, analytical mind – sometimes with a degree to prove it. But to the

professional telephone salesperson, no proof is needed. His incise questioning quickly categorises him.

With this buyer, you must be ultra-careful of the claims and statements you make. No salesperson should exaggerate, although many do, perhaps unwittingly. For example:

> 'It is noiseless, Mr. Smith.'
> The logical buyer immediately answers:
> 'If it were noiseless, it wouldn't work at all. There must be some sound from it.'

That sort of retort can set a saleperson right back in his chair.

Here is another example:

> 'That means, Mr. Smith, that the interest rate works out at 14%, and it is tax free.'
> 'Can you guarantee that? It is only correct under present legislation. Are you able to assure me that there will be no change in the law within the next ten years?'

And bang goes the sale on an investment plan.

The logical buyer must be sold to logically, and there should be no attempt to appeal to his emotions. Any claim which cannot be justified must not be made. A statement must not be so embellished as to give him the opportunity to criticise a minor point of your claim. For example:

- 'Everyone believes it,'
- 'It is a well-known fact in the trade . . .'
- 'It applies particularly to you in your profession . . .'

These remarks enable the logical buyer to interrupt with:

'Why do you say in my profession? Doesn't it apply just as much to men and women in all walks of life?'

Neither should you deal in approximations. Try to be exact. He will want to know exact costings, correct measurements, delivery dates which are not guesswork.

Although he will demand the fullest details, remember *you must not give them to him over the telephone*. The fact that he wants more evidence is an ideal opening for you. It is the reason why you want to make an appointment to see him.

With Mr. Logical, cut out all the padding. Give him information which is logical enough for him to give you an appointment.

The Semi-Tycoon

Most people think of the tycoon as the dynamic head of a self-built empire, but generally the people we meet when we sell are only half or two-thirds of the way up the ladder of success. Yet they like to act the part of the big boss, which is why they are called semi-tycoons.

They are often difficult to contact on the telephone and treat telephone salespeople as if they were one of their junior staff. If you request an appointment, he will fob you off onto one of his assistants, just to show how important he is.

Standard ego-building techniques don't work well with him, although they may with his manager. With a semi-tycoon, you use the *maybe you are not so great* technique.

At the approach, for example, you could say:

'Mr. Johnson, I am not quite certain whether you handle communications networks or whether I should speak to Ms. Saunders (his superior) about it.'

If it is suggested to the semi-tycoon that he has not the

power to buy when he is the buyer, he will indulge in ego-building. He will not want to approach his boss and will make it clear that he is the man who makes the decisions. You must then be ready with a subsidiary question to stimulate the semi-tycoon's thinking and arouse his interest. The rules are:

- Allow him to build himself up.
- Ask questions to stimulate his thinking.
- Do not waste his time by asking questions which serve no purpose.
- Let him believe that he is controlling the conversation.

The Complaining Buyer
The attacking complainer is the person who, as soon as you speak to him, says:

- 'You're just the person I want to speak to. That last delivery of yours was so badly packed that the contents arrived damaged. They were unsaleable.'
- 'Give you an interview? I told your sales manager six months ago that I wouldn't do any more business with you.'
- 'The ad didn't pull at all. I certainly wouldn't repeat it in your paper.'

We now are not dealing with a buyer who has a genuine complaint. We covered the problems of handling such a person in Chapters 8 and 9 on incoming and outgoing calls. The complaining buyer uses his complaint as a defensive weapon. He does not specifically pick you out for a fight. He uses the technique with every salesperson he doesn't want to see or give an order.

It makes him immediate master of the situation, which

makes it easier for him to turn down your request for an interview or order.

Once you have classified the complainer, and have made the appropriate notes in your diary, you can prepare yourself for him. It is of little use explaining to such a man that the goods were packed perfectly or that, because he wanted credit for goods he couldn't sell, *he* was in the wrong, not the manager.

There is one effective way of handling this man. Let him first complain, and don't interrupt. Apologise – it won't help, but it is courteous – then offer him something special:

- 'It is because we have let you down that I am telephoning you. I want to put things right. This is what I will do specially for you . . .'

The next time you call, don't give him the opportunity to complain, but say to him immediately:

- 'Mr. Smith, I am sure you have no further reason to complain about . . . I am looking after your requirements personally.'

Whatever you do, you must not emphasise the complaint, but neither must you ignore it. The rule, then, is to *apologise briefly and then sell very hard on the special service you are offering him.*

There are only two occasions in selling when a customer's words are almost brushed side. One is when he raises a frivolous objection, and the other when both of you know that it is his standard practice to attack by complaining.

The Buying Bully

Bully buyers are few in number. They must not be compared with the sarcastic buyer or the rude buyer.

The bully buyer delights in squashing a salesperson. She has her own coterie of suppliers who fawn upon her or have a friendly relationship with her outside business. She gives the appearance of affability and she is usually a good mixer in pubs and clubs.

She often tries to be boss at home, but rarely succeeds, and psychologists might conclude that this is one of the reasons why she likes bullying salespeople. But, like all bullies, she is a coward at heart and has to be handled firmly. It is no use kow-towing to her. If you have to do that, it is far better to end the call and try someone else, because you will never win.

You must be prepared for her offensive manner. She will also want to do all the talking and will bait you about the quality of your goods and the prices you charge.

This person is not difficult to handle. You must not contradict her – not until you are well in with her, anyway – because that is just what she is waiting for to allow her to explode.

Keep on plugging away at your benefits. The more she shouts, the more you talk benefits, and never sound apologetic. Use such sentences as:

- 'You are a person who can make up your mind quickly. This is well-known in the trade, and this special line is just what you are looking for. You will also want quick delivery.'
- 'You will forgive me for saying this, Ms. Johnson – you are known as a tough buyer, but you are also known as a very fair-minded person, so you will allow me to explain . . .'
- If 'What do you want?' is her opening greeting, say:
- 'We both want the same thing, Ms. Johnson – extra

cash, extra security, extra savings. All I want is five minutes of your time. If, after five minutes have passed, you don't want me to stay, I'll go. Is that fair?'

The Indecisive Buyer

Most of us complain from time to time about the lack of attention given to us by shop assistants. They, in turn, have a case, however, for sometimes feeling that they would like to karate-chop down certain customers – the indecisive customer, for instance, who will pick up this and that, show an interest in one colour and then another, be certain that Y is exactly what they want, and then remind themselves that K might be more suitable. It is not that they are timid or frightened to buy; it is just that they are indecisive.

You will talk to many buyers like this on the telephone. They will call you to place an order and then be beset by a hundred doubts, while you have other customers waiting on the line. You will make a superb presentation and feel certain that the order is yours, and then he will hum and ha and if and but.

You will always have to make the final decision for the indecisive buyer. Otherwise, he will be continually evasive, and will utilise a whole list of excuses to help him, e.g.:
- 'I'll talk to my partner.'
- 'I'll consult my solicitor.'
- 'I'll definitely have it later on.'

When the indecisive buyer shows a preference, you must make his mind up for him, and forget all the other articles in the range.

When the PA hesitates to make an appointment for

her manager, you must make the decision for her.

You may wish to say, e.g.:

- 'I appreciate, Mrs. Jones, that you are not certain of Mr. Wilkins' movements at the moment, but I'll risk that. Make it three o'clock – you did think he might be free then – and if I call and he can't see me, that's my bad luck.'
- 'You like the small size better – I'll send you a gross.'
- 'You won't have any worry, Mr. Brown. Our actuaries have worked it all out for you and you know the high reputation of my company. You only have to tell us the amount that you can afford. £20,000 too high? Right, let's make it £18,000.'

With the indecisive buyer, you must act as his best adviser. Never let him down and you have a customer for life.

The Talkative Buyer

If you are not allowed to give your presentation, how can you close an order or get an interview?

To prevent you from completing your sales sequence, one type of buyer keeps talking. The sale is bogged down. Because you understand the importance of good human relations, you may have asked the prospect if he enjoyed his holiday; the prospect will then talk about his holiday for so long that there is little time left for selling. There is only time for the prospect to say, 'Call me next month.'

This type of prospect or customer will sidetrack in all sorts of ways, and the salesperson cannot stem the flow of words. While you must not be a pouncer and interrupt a buyer, there is a vast difference between pouncing and allowing a buyer to take control.

With Mr. Talker, you must interrupt the prospect

without offending him. You must wait until he says something that can be linked to a sales point. He might be explaining how the weather has affected his business. You interrupt:

'Excuse me, Mr. Brown, I know you will agree that it is when the weather is bad and your customers stay at home that you have to do something to bring them into the shop. This is where I can help you . . .'

The talker may be interminably describing some technicality of his manufacturing process. He is bogging down in technical details. You interrupt:

'It is obvious why you are technically so far ahead of your competitors. I can help you to beat them on price. May I call . . .'

The talker will only quieten down when he appreciates your strength and that of your proposal.

The Too-Friendly Buyer

A buyer may be abrupt, curt, almost rude, yet he may still listen to your proposition. The too-friendly buyer, however, can make life difficult. She agrees with everything in a facile way.

Her pleasant manner is a disguise. She knows it is hard for you to tie her down while she is being so friendly. The timid salesperson is always impressed with friendliness, and is easily put off.

It takes a strong salesperson to overcome the too-friendly buyer; his strength will enable him to put his foot down and start to sell. If the customer agrees with him, he will ask for the order. When she doesn't agree, he will sell even more strongly.

The salesperson knows this buyer for what she is worth and will not be sidetracked by her friendliness. Even at the risk of antagonising her, the strong salesperson will carry on with his sequence.

You must win the friendship of a buyer, but the best proof of her friendship is when she gives you orders.

The Timid Buyer

The timid buyer cannot make a decision easily, and takes avoiding action. He should not really be a buyer at all. The more timid the buyer, the more decisive you must be. Do not give him alternatives; his mind must be made up for him. He must be given a single course of action, and induced to take it.

The timid buyer's greatest anxiety is that he will make a mistake. This is understandable in a very small business where a mistake could cause considerable financial embarrassment, but big store buyers, too, can be timid. They are scared of the merchandising manager's displeasure if they purchase the wrong stock. They are frightened of overstocking. They are afraid of opening new accounts.

Time must be spent on building Mr. Timid's confidence – confidence in you and your products. This must be accompanied by tremendous enthusiasm. Some of this will, eventually, rub off on Mr. Timid, who will then summon up the courage to place an order on the telephone, or to make an appointment.

Talk to Mr. Timid of larger quantities than you hope to sell. He may be frightened at first, but when you then suggest a smaller quantity, he will be relieved, and more inclined to buy.

The Silent Buyer

While the talker won't stop talking, his opposite number won't say anything. When the salesperson explains the main benefit, the only answer she gets is a grunt.

You must make this kind of prospect agree with you. He must be brought into the sale. Even the most vociferous salesperson cannot overcome the silent buyer and will eventually dry up.

The way to succeed is to sell by using a series of questions. Practically every sentence must be a question. At first, your answer may be a grunt, but eventually the prospect must say something. He might be able to grunt a half-dozen times, but on the seventh occasion, tough as he is, the prospect must answer.

Ask questions, and soon the silent buyer will begin to talk. When he starts talking, you know you are making progress.

The Bluffer

The bluffer is similar to Mr. Timid at heart. He deceives salespeople. He talks in large quantities, stresses that he buys in thousands, but he always delays making a decision.

Mr. Bluffer says:

'I don't believe in playing about. When I buy, I buy. It's not worth my while opening an account with you for just a few hundred. In six months' time, I should be ready to give you a good order. Telephone me then.'

This is bluff. You must tie him down. He may want to place a small order but, having taken his stand, he cannot easily reduce the quantity. Say to him,

'Mr. Johnson, I appreciate that you want to buy two thousand but if you will take my advice, don't. Two thousand would not worry you, but it would worry me. One of my biggest accounts began in quite a small way. The buyer is a man like you, who knows his own mind, but I asked him to test out the market and find out for himself just how many he could sell in the course of six weeks. If you would begin with five hundred . . .'

The chances are that you will get your small order, but if you wait a month or two to obtain the big contract, you probably will be sadly disillusioned.

You must tie the bluffer down to a small quantity initially, even if it goes against the grain. The big business will come later, after his confidence in your products has been proved right.

The Stubborn Buyer

When the stubborn buyer has made up her mind, nothing seems to budge her. Any hint of criticism will lose the order. She would rather make a wrong decision than change her mind. Her problem is psychological. She is afraid of appearing weak. If she has raised an objection, she doesn't want you to prove her wrong. She is the kind of person who will tell you that she believes in admitting when she is wrong. Unfortunately, she always believes that she is right. The strength of your sales presentation enables you to sell to her. A presentation that forestalls objections lets her feel she is making all the decisions, all the time.

To know yourself, and to know your buyer, are excellent twin objectives for all salespeople.

CHAPTER 12

The Professional Salesperson

Whenever the telephone rings in a shop, office, factory, store or warehouse, there is a sales opportunity – an opportunity to create goodwill, to close a sale, to handle an enquiry effectively or to calm an irate customer. When anyone picks up the telephone to call a customer or prospect, the same opportunities arise.

In the same way as salesmanship has improved so much over the years, so will the standard of service given to customers by those who use the telephone.

Modern sales professionals have high IQs, are ambitious and work hard. They are also keen to improve their general knowledge of business. They not only attend courses on selling, but, in ever-increasing numbers, they go to courses covering such subjects as inventory management, credit control, accountancy, management, presentation skills, proposal writing . . .

AND TELEPHONE SELLING.

And that is what this book is all about . . .

Index

TACK TRAINING

Alfred Tack was the founder of the world-renowned training consultancy which bears his name. TACK courses are run in over 40 countries and 25 languages, covering such topics as:

■ **FINANCE**
Financial Understanding for the
    Senior Executive
Introduction to Finance for
    Managers

■ **MANAGEMENT AND SUPERVISORY**
Leadership in Senior
    Management
The Multi-Discipline Manager
Motivational Leadership
Effective Supervisory
    Management
Effective Office Management
Time Management for Managers
Recruitment Interviewing and
    Selection
Performance Appraisal

■ **COMMUNICATION**
Successful Business
    Presentations
Training the Trainer

■ **SALES**
Sales Training
Selling to Industry and Commerce
Advanced Sales Development
Profitable Negotiating
Professional Telephone Selling
Customer Service by Telephone
Selling Financial Services
Customer Relations for Service
    Engineers

■ **MARKETING AND SALES MANAGEMENT**
Introduction to Marketing
Strategic Marketing in Action
Field Sales Management
Profitable Sales Management

In-Company Training is provided in all these areas, specially designed to suit specific client requirements.

Open Courses are run regularly on most of the above topics, with mixed attendance by client companies from all areas of industry and commerce.

TACK TRAINING INTERNATIONAL
TACK House, Latimer Park, Chesham, BUCKS, HP5 1TR U.K.
Telephone (+44) 1494 766611   www.tack.co.uk

**Vermilion Books may be obtained
from any good bookshop
or by telephoning TBS Direct on:
01206 255 800.**